Teach'n Beginning Defensive Basketball Drills, Plays, and Games Free Flow Handbook

By
Bob Swope

Series 5, Vol. 12 Free Flow Paperback Edition
Copyright 2014 Bob Swope
ISBN 13: 9780991115181

TABLE OF CONTENTS

1. Warning

If your kids, players on your team, or the participants have any physically limiting conditions, bleeding disorder, high blood pressure, any kind of heart condition, pregnancy or any other condition that may limit them physically, you should have them check with their doctor before letting them participate in any of the drills, plays, games, activities, or exercises discussed in this book.

Be sure participants in these drills, plays, games, or exercises that might make hard contact with any of the other participants are all approximately of the same weight and size to avoid a possible injury.

All of the drills, plays, exercises, and games for kids discussed in this book should be supervised by a competent adult, coach, or a professional using any required equipment and safety procedures. **AUTHOR ASSUMES NO LIABILITY FOR ANY ACCIDENTAL INJURY OR EVEN DEATH THAT MAY RESULT FROM USING ANY OF THE BASKETBALL TECHNIQUES DISCUSSED IN THS BOOK.**

Extra care and caution should be taken with any of the drills in this book where players may accidentally get hit with any thrown or passed basketballs while using the drills discussed in this book. Especially where a hard thrown ball is coming right at the player, or a player jumping up to block or rebound can come down hard on a players head, because these may be the more dangerous things to watch for. Also watch for over exertion (heat stroke and heart problems) to any of your kids or players on a hot court or a hot day, Having a "defibrillator" near by would be a big help just in case something happens.

Bob Swope
Jacobob Press LLC
Publisher

2

2. Introduction

My Interest and Intent

Occasionally youth basketball coaches have asked me about basic Defensive drills, plays, strategies, tactics and games that would be good to have all in one book, to use for training purposes. This handbook is intended to be a supplemental book to my "Teach'n Basketball" book. It is orientated more for the beginner basketball coach, rather than parents at home teaching fundamentals. However, parents can help their kids by getting them to work on the drills, plays, tactics, and strategies in this book. We will break this down into where your players are in their training, and what they are doing at that stage of their training. Also what drills, strategies, plays and tactics to use that will accomplish your goals in teaching them. My suggestion is use the time you have each week to maximize what you want to teach. For the younger 6 -11 years of age kids it's better to break practice drills down into more than one small group to keep everyone busy so that they don't get bored. This is not always easy to do because many coaches only want things done their way, and they don't always trust a helper assistant to do it their way. However, sooner or later you need to trust assistants to help get more done. It's in the best interest of the kids.

3. Discussion

Training Sessions

Some of the beginning basketball practices I've seen will only last about an hour and 30 minutes at most. However it's usually only 1 hour. This is where one coach has the whole group. I have seen coaches spending 15 to 20 minutes warming up and stretching. That leaves only 40 to 70 or so minutes to instruct, not counting the water breaks. And it's not-always one-on one instruction. This means you need to manage your time efficiently. You should limit the warm-up and stretching, so you can utilize the whole practice time. The other thing that is important is how many times a week is your practice. If it's only one day a week, you better sit down and make a schedule, so you can cover all the things they need to learn. Then follow it. If you have more time, like two hours, you can teach even more fundamentals.

Time
Generally keep your training time to around 15 minutes per drill being explained, especially if you have a group unless otherwise noted. Now here is where your training techniques may need to change. If you have a helper you can split into two groups. As an example, you might be teaching "guarding" and your assistant "rebounding." Then after 10 minutes you switch or rotate groups. This is because traditionally there is a lot of techniques to teach to beginning kids. In other words always keep your kids busy doing something at all times except for water breaks. Don't have any kids just standing around waiting because there is only one coach. You don't get as much teaching in that way, within any one practice. Also young kids traditionally get bored easily if you don't keep them busy for the entire training session.

Session Suggestions
I suggest getting as many assistant coaches as you can, then explain to them individually what they are responsible for teaching at their station. Tell your staff to learn all the kids names the first day if possible. Time wise plan your whole practice session. The kids will learn more in the short periods of time you have for teaching each day or week. As for the teaching methods we suggest using the "IDEA" slogan approach. **I**ntroduce, **D**emonstrate, **E**xplain what you are teaching, and **A**ttend to all the players in the group.

The Opponent
If it's possible, it could be beneficial to understand what tendencies your opponent has. Your players need to learn how to quickly figure out what their opponent is doing against them offensively. Your players should recognize the importance of this strategy, especially after playing an opponent more than once. Here is a little strategy you can employ as their coach. Keep a small pad of paper in your pocket and take notes. Look for

weaknesses, then when it's game time, you can pick the offensive strategies that will attack, counterattack, and defeat what the opponent is doing. Start teaching your young players to have a defensive game plan before they go into a game, then test them to make sure and remember what it is. Also have a back up plans in case your first plan didn't work and you need to change or modify your plans and tactics.

Pre Practice/Game Warm Up

Before your team starts to practice or get in a game, they need to go through a little warm up to get their muscles warmed up and stretched out. We will give you a nice little quick warm up routine to use. 10 minutes should do it. Once your kids learn it, they can do it on their own as a group. If you can teach them to do this well, and look good at it, your opponent may be impressed or intimidated by your teams discipline and focus. The organized warm up may put you at an advantage, as your opponent's may be a little psyched out.

Drills

I am going to refer to the drills as "Skill Training Activities" because that's what they really are. Also I am going to throw in a newer term now being used a lot. It is called "Core Training". What it does is train their body to make certain moves that will make them a better player. Drills will be organized by *"numbers"* so that your assistant coaches can use them and become more familiar with them that way. This way you are all on the same page as they say.

Techniques

For easy reference the techniques will be organized by *"numbers"* also. They will be arranged in the different defensive techniques and tactics. Each technique or tactic will have a short explanation for how it is supposed to work, strong points, what it is designed to accomplish.

Game Type Scrimmages

It's a good idea to introduce game type scrimmages once in a while. Beginners sometimes have a tendency to get bored with constant drilling. They want to see what it's like to go out and play in a game against an actual opponent. You need to referee these games just like in a real game. Just don't get frustrated by expecting perfect play by beginners. Have several spotters, each watching some particular aspect of their defensive play. As they get better you can be more particular about calling scores and penalties.

Core Training Games

Many coaches over the years have asked me to give them some "core training" games they can have the kids play once in a while at practices. Not just any games though, but games that will help develop their "core training" and "muscle memory" in a particular skill. So we are adding some games that will do just that. For easy reference these games will be organized by "*numbers*" also. Some of the time it's hard for coaches to buy into these games, but the more you play them, the more you will see your player's agility, speed and skills improving. Each game will have a short explanation for how it is supposed to work, strong points, and what the game is designed to accomplish.

4. Strategies and Tactics

The first strategy I recommend is "have a game plan" to match your team with their opponent. Try to watch their opponent warming up, and make some notes. Remember though these are only kids, so coach accordingly with your strategies and tactics if you are working with kids 7-11 years of age. You know the old "KISS" (Keep-It-Simple-Stupid) phrase. In advanced levels of basketball the players have special offensive roles to play. However, for beginners it's important to teach them that everyone on the court plays offense and defense. Here are just a few very basic strategies and some tactics you can use for young beginning teams that: should prove to be helpful.

Defense

Basic Team Strategies and Concepts

1. If you have a team of young players that are not too good with their defensive techniques or skills have them all work on their weakest skill or skills at home around the garage basket every chance they get.
2. Teach your players that defense is also based on a teamwork concept, not just a lot of individual star players stealing the ball and grabbing all the rebounds.
3. Figure out if your opponents are using a "possession style" or "fast break style" of offense, then coach your team accordingly.
5. The minute your team loses offensive possession of the ball teach them to transition quickly and be ready to defend the "space" through and behind their defense.
6. If you have a big tall center, and the other team does not, then put your center near the basket in the lo- post, and let them block shots and grab rebounds. Teach them to jump _way up_ when they rebound, they will have a better chance of getting the ball than if they stand there under the basket flat footed waiting for the ball to come down.
7. If you have one of the faster teams in your division, then use a fast pressure defense, and a full court press when allowed.
8. If your team is good at ball handling, and quickness, then you can use just about any of the defenses, depending on who you are playing, and what their strengths are.

Individual Strategies and Concepts

1. Tell your players to not try to do too much all by themselves, just learn and do their job on defense.
2. Teach your players to always look at the ball and not the player, especially their eyes. This way they won't get faked out as often
3. When they are sitting on the bench or in position waiting for the play to come to them, tell them to be alert at noticing what the players attacking them are doing. Look for a weakness.

4. Tell them to learn how to become quick with their hands when guarding, and be the best ball handler they can be.

Beginners Simple Defensive Role Playing Strategies

1. Each player has a basic role to play and a position on the court to maintain. Once you have assigned your players to a position have them learn the role they play at that position.
2. Guards are out in front. Their basic job is guard the opposing teams guards and don't get by or pass. They are usually smaller and faster.
3. Forwards move down the court usually to the outside or around the edge of the key and guard the opposing teams forwards. They are usually bigger, taller, fast, good jumpers, and rebounders.
4. Centers are usually right around or under the basket. But sometimes they play a high post at the top of the key. Their role is usually to keep the opposing teams players far out from the basket, breaking to the basket, their hands are up to block shots, and they try to grab all the rebounds if possible. Not always, but usually, they are one of the tallest players on the team.

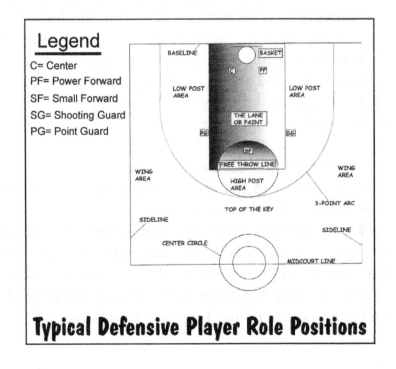

Typical Defensive Player Role Positions

Other Tactics and Styles of Play
There are other styles of play for offense. What style you play will depend on you and what style of defense you are comfortable with as a coach. However, you should know about some of these because if you have the right players it could make your team or players better. These styles do vary quite a bit all over the world though. It will come down to what your players are capable of.
Basic Defensive Styles
Half Court:
1. Man-to-Man Pressure
2. Out of Bounds Man-to-Man
3. Zone
4. Delay

Full Court:
1. Zone Press
2. Fast Break Transition
3. Tip Off

Further along in the book we will give the different plays you can run in each one of these different styles. And we will explain how they work.

5. Warm Up Exercises

I'm going to give you a quick warm up routine you can use to get your kids warmed up and their muscles stretched. Teach your players how to do these group exercises all by themselves. Here is an idea I have used before. When you are warming up your team, you can try this. Have your captain or a respected teammate stand in front of the group, and lead the routine. Teach your players to count slowly and out loud. The team alternates counting, when the leaders yell. "One," the group yells, "Two," etc. You only need to do six reps of each exercise. It's really a "psyche out" for any opponent's watching. And you may need this edge if the opponent's are more experienced or stronger players. You are only looking at about 10 minutes to go through these.

Jumping Jacks	Hamsrtings /Quads	Pelvics	Ankles
Front Quadriceps	Rear Shoulders	Front Shoulders	Calf

The Simple Routine

1. Start by doing 10 jumping jacks to get their muscles warmed up.
2. Next slowly do 6 "seated hamstring/quadriceps stretches.
3. Next slowly do 3 pelvic stretches on each side, holding for 3 seconds between them.
4. Next slowly do 6 push forward pull back ankle stretches.
5. Next slowly do 3 front quadriceps stretches on both thighs, leaning forward and holding for 3 seconds between them.
6. Next slowly do 6 rear shoulder stretches, holding for 3 seconds.
7. Next slowly do 3 front shoulder stretches on each shoulder, holding for 3 seconds between them.
8. Last use a teammate, or find a wall, and slowly do 3 calf stretches on each leg, holding it 3 seconds between them.

6. Defensive Skill Training Activities

Note: ALL ACTIVITIES will be numbered for "EASY " reference.

The defensive drills will cover all the types of skills that young kids learning to play defensive basketball need to know to get started off on the right foot. Some are "Core Training" and most all involve "Muscle Memory" training. They train the body, arms, legs and feet of your players to make certain moves and decisions that will make them a better player. Defensive players have to be poised, and patient. The guards see the whole court and they talk to their teammates. Basically they try to keep the opponents front players from moving the ball down the court and attempting to make baskets, or set up teammates to shoot them.

The skill activities are numbered so that you can have your assistant coach(s) use them and become more familiar with them for reference purposes. These skill activities will cover the very basic fundaments like pressing, guarding, blocking shots, stealing the ball, and rebounding. We will also try to cover some of the little special techniques that will help them. The plan is stay with small training groups, where you or one of your coaches is teaching one of these skills. Keep the time period short, maybe 10 minutes on the group to group activities. Then blow a whistle and one group moves over to the next group of training (rotating).

The size of your groups will depend on how many kids you have in your training session, and how many instructors (coaches) you have. As an example if you have 12 kids on your team, then you could have 2 groups of 6. Then you would need 2 stations and at least one instructor or coach per group. The bigger your group is though the more problems you will have. Smaller groups mean more touches, and more teaching control on your part. However, some drills may need to be combined for bigger groups in order to teach similar techniques in a team group more smoothly and quicker. If you can find them, have an instructor and an assistant at each station, then show them what to do. Most coaches don't like to do this even if they may need to because of a large group size and fear of losing control, but using parents as assistants and showing them exactly what you want them to do can work. I do this all the time and it works great for me with young kids. Parents are usually just sitting around watching with nothing to do anyway, so why not get them involved and put them to work. Also then they will appreciate more the training you are giving them. You would be surprised at how many parents are willing to help, not a lot but quite a few. And that's all you need. Just show them *EXACTLY* what you want them to do. That's the key.

Here is another technique that works great with young kids. They have a short attention span. So when you need to just talk to all of them, then make them sit down cross legged, Indian style, or take a knee, and in a semi circle around in front of you. When you do it this way, they have less of a tendency to mess around, especially with boys, who talk too much when you are talking . Don't let them stand up, that's when the listening usually tends to stop and distractions set in.

Additional Help for Activities

If you are a beginning coach, and you are having trouble understanding how to implement these offensive activities in more detail, get a copy of our "Teach'n Basketball" book. This is our in depth teaching book for basketball, and it goes into a little more detail on exactly how to teach kids the particular skill we are discussing.

Legend for All Diagrams
(Unless otherwise spelled out in the diagram or section)

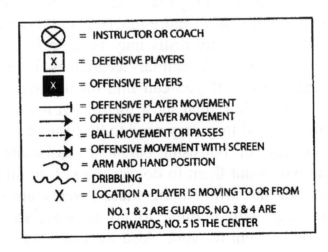

⊗	= INSTRUCTOR OR COACH
X	= DEFENSIVE PLAYERS
X	= OFFENSIVE PLAYERS
⊢——	= DEFENSIVE PLAYER MOVEMENT
——→	= OFFENSIVE PLAYER MOVEMENT
----→	= BALL MOVEMENT OR PASSES
——⊣	= OFFENSIVE MOVEMENT WITH SCREEN
⌒o	= ARM AND HAND POSITION
∿∿	= DRIBBLING
X	= LOCATION A PLAYER IS MOVING TO OR FROM

NO. 1 & 2 ARE GUARDS, NO. 3 & 4 ARE
FORWARDS, NO. 5 IS THE CENTER

Basic Defensive Skills

GUARDING

Learning the different ways to guard an opposing player is a very important part of the defensive game. If an offensive player is allowed to go up the court unguarded, they will probably end up making a basket. Really it is defense that win games. And defense is guarding. I think the trick in guarding a player is stay real close to them, but go out of the way not to touch them. And the way to learn how to do this is, lots of practice, over and over, with supervision. Several things to remember are always raise both hands straight up when the player has stopped and it looks like they are going to pass the ball. And don't look into the opposing players eyes because it makes it easier for them to fake you as to which direction they are going to go and what they are going to do. If you teach your players to look at the ball while they are dribbling instead of their eyes, they will not be faked out as easily. The other thing to remember is, have them always keep their body between the opposing player and the basket. The following drills are all designed to help give them the skills needed to guard a player.

Skill Activity (No.1) Defensive Stance
Object of the activity: Teach all your players how to get into a defensive stance for guarding.
What you will need:
You will need a little room on the corner of the court, a basketball, a coach, and a whistle.
The Basics Are:
This stance gets them ready for whatever the opponent might do. U.C.L.A.'s great coach, John Wooden, constantly stressed this stance for his players. Many coaches like this stance because it allows the defender to cover a larger area very quickly. One foot is forward, but it doesn't really matter which one, except when an opponent is being guarded along the "baseline", or "sideline". In that case, the forward foot must be the foot closest to the line. This is to cut off the side lines as a possible

driving lane to the basket. The other foot is back. Your weight needs to be evenly distributed on the balls of their feet. The body is bent at the waist, with the knees flexed and loose. The forward hand is raised and extended toward the opponent. This is to distract them, and block their vision. The other hand is at waist level, ready to block the passing lane on that side *(SEE FIGURE 1)*.

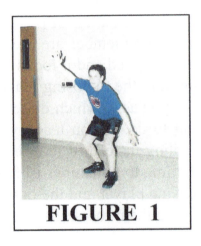

FIGURE 1

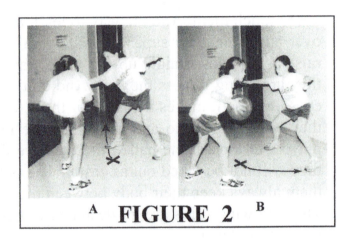

A **FIGURE 2** B

If the opponent starts to dribble around their right side, they pivot off their left foot, and take a long step back with the right foot, right along the path of where the opponent will be making their drive. The right hand reaches out to cut off the dribble or a possible pass *(SEE FIGURE 2-A)*. If the opponent starts to dribble around their left side, they pivot off their right foot, and take a long step back with the left foot, right along the path of where the opponent will be making their drive. The left hand reaches, and swings out to cut off the dribble or a possible pass *(SEE FIGURE 2-B)*. All players need to work on this drill, to improve on their defense.

Working the activity:
To practice this have them go out to the court, or driveway, and get into their defensive stance *(SEE FIGURE 1)*. Then you get about 6 feet in front of them, with a basketball, and slowly start to dribble right at them.

When you are about 3 feet away, then make a sudden break, and try to dribble around them to the right. What they need to do is quickly pivot off their left foot, turn to the right, and take a long step back with their right foot. As they do this, they have to reach out with their right hand, down low and block your dribble path. When they do block your path, be careful, and don't hurt them by running hard into them. Remember, this is practice. Just stop when they have effectively blocked your path. After doing this several times, around their right side, then switch and try to go around the left side. While doing all of this try to watch and see if they are pivoting, and stepping off the correct foot.

Emphasize: Getting the correct hand up and the other one down depending on which side of them the opponent tries to move in.

Run this activity: for about 10 minutes and making sure each player gets at least 5 attempts at guarding you. If players are not catching on have an assistant coach pull them aside and show them what they are doing wrong so that the practice does not stop and keeps going.

Skill Activity (No.2) The Shuffle Slide Side Step
Object of the activity: Teach all your players how to make the shuffle slide side step to stay in front of the player they are guarding.
What you will need:
You will need a little room on the corner of the court, 2 players, a basketball, a coach, and a whistle.
The Basics Are:
When they are backing up the court, and guarding a player as they come up the court, tell them to make sure to stay low and slide sideways when they try to go around you. While maintaining a position in front of them, you should get into a "ready position." Your feet should be shoulder width apart, knees bent, hands outstretched in front of you with palms up, and elbows slightly bent *(SEE FIGURE 3).* Make sure that you teach them to never cross over step with their feet if they have to move sideways, they slide shuffle sideways instead, to stay in front of the player they are guarding. This is where this drill comes in if they are "guards," or "small forwards." It is to get them used to sliding sideways.

FIGURE 3

Working the activity:
To practice this have them go out to the court or driveway, or even in the back yard, and get into their defensive stance (ready position). Then you, or a coach, stand in front of them and move sideways as if dribbling the ball ***(SEE FIGURE 3)***. They have to shuffle slide sideways all the way across the court, or driveway, to one side then all the way back across to the other side. They have to do this while staying directly in front of you. "Guards" should do this drill every day for at least 10 minutes. The <u>*TIP*</u> here is, stay low with the knees always bent and with the back straight up.

Emphasize: Always shuffle side step never crossover their foot.

Run this activity: for about 10 minutes and making sure each player gets at least 5 attempts at guarding you while shuffle slide stepping. If players are not catching on have an assistant coach pull them aside and show them what they are doing wrong so that the practice does not stop and keeps going.

Skill Activity (No.4 to 6) Boxing Out

Object of the activity: Teach all your players how to box out opponents to keep them from getting to the ball or a rebound.

What you will need:

You will need a little room around the basket, 2 players, a basketball, a coach, and a whistle.

The Basics Are:

This drill is for "centers" and "power forwards". They play mostly in the low post, next to the basket. What you have to teach them to do is play right in back of the opposing center, or power forward blocking their path to the basket. While in that position they can put their hand on the back of the player, but don't lean on them, push them or restrict them from moving ***(SEE FIGURE 5)***. This is where strength comes in. The center and power forwards have to be fast enough to get back down the court on defense, and get into their defensive position. They use the strength of their feet, and lower body, to not let the opposing player back up, or push them toward the basket. "Boxing out" is when the opposing player turns, and makes a shot over your hands stretched straight up, then you whirl around quickly and put your back to them. Then you put both arms out to the side to keep the opponent from getting around you for the rebound ***(SEE FIGURE 4)***. This keeps them from going to the basket for any possible rebound or tip in shot.. Sometimes this is called "blocking out".

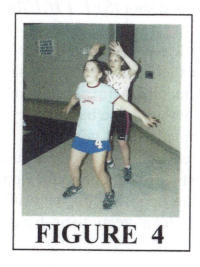

FIGURE 4

FIGURE 5

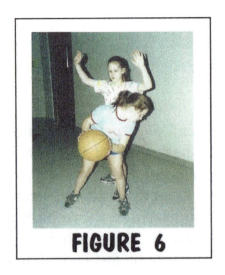

FIGURE 6

Working the activity:
To practice this drill, have your player go out about 5 feet in front of the basket, and to the right side. Then get into a defensive "ready position." Then you, or a coach, get in front of them with a basketball, and turn so your back is facing the basket. Make sure they put their hand on your back then you pivot, turn, and try to shoot a basket over the top of them, or around them. When they see that you are going to turn and try to shoot, they have to stay right with you, outstretch their hands straight up, and try to keep you from getting a good shot *(SEE FIGURE 6)*.

Next, right after they see the ball leave your hand, they need to whirl around and put their hands out to their sides, face the basket, and box (block) you out from getting around them to get any rebounds *(SEE FIGURE 4)*. Then if the ball does not go in the basket, they have to jump up for the rebound. You should practice this with them for at least 10 minutes at a time, and from different spots in an arc around the basket. The *TIP* here is, have them stay just close enough to the opposing player, so they don't foul them. And if the opposing player wants to run into your son or daughter, then have them keep their hands up without

18

fouling, lean back, hold their position, and let the opposing player take a charging foul into them. And explain to them that when they see the player is going to shoot then always have them get at least one, if not two hands, way up high in front of the opposing player to distract them.

Emphasize: The whirling around and boxing out at just the right time, and then going up for the rebound.

Run this activity: for about 10 minutes and making sure each player gets at least 5 attempts at boxing out. If players are not catching on have an assistant coach pull them aside and show them what they are doing wrong so that the practice does not stop and keeps going.

Defensive Skill Training Activities (Drills)

ALL DRILLS will be numbered for "EASY" reference.

Explanation

These defensive drills will cover guarding, stealing, rebounding, and shot blocking. Some are fundamental technique drills and some are team drills. We won't have every drill ever invented, but we will pick some of the better ones for little kids, and give you some choices. It is recommended that use of these drills be kept to a 10 minute time limit for the little kids depending on how much time you have for practice. You can use a whistle to start and stop the drill. Then all players rotate to the next group. You are going to be working them hard so plan for short water breaks periodically every 1/2 hour or so.

GUARDING DRILLS

Skill Activity (No.144) The Sideline to Sideline Shuffle/Slide Drill
Object of the activity: Teach all your players how to do the shuffle/slide step for longer distances. This is "Core Training" and "muscle Memory" training.
What you will need:

You will need half the court, 2 groups of players, 2 basketballs, 2 coaches, and a whistle.

The Basics Are:

This drill uses the shuffle/slide step as in Skill Activity 2. Making this move across court will really help them stay with opponents while guarding them.

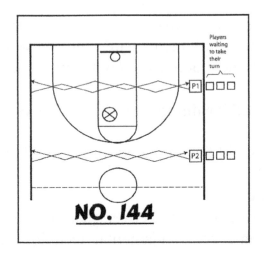

NO. 144

Working the activity:

Have your players line up on one side of the half court in 2 lines. The front players P1 and P2 get into their defensive stance and start slide shuffling sideways across the court. The object is to stay low all the way across and back, then go to the end of the line. They keep their arms held out wide, and they have to slap the floor about every 3 steps with both hands. This is core training to teach their body to stay low. Depending on their age and how many players you have you may only want to run this drill for 5 to 10 minutes. And you may want to run this drill just to **center court and back** for the little kids. It's an energy draining drill so that should be enough for them.

Emphasize: The quick feet and using the arm for balance. Have them try to go just a little faster each time.

Run this activity: for about 5 to10 minutes and making sure each player gets at least 2 attempts at shuffle/sliding all the way across and back. If players are not catching on have an assistant coach pull them aside and show them what they are doing wrong so that the practice does not stop and keeps going.

Skill Activity (No.145) The Guarding the Dribbler Drill
Object of the activity: Teach all your players how to guard dribbling opponents for long distances.
What you will need:
You will need half the court, 2 groups of players split half to a side, 2 basketballs, 2 coaches, and 2 whistles.
The Basics Are:
This drill uses the shuffle/slide step as in Skill Activity 2. Making this move across court will really help them stay with opponents while guarding them.

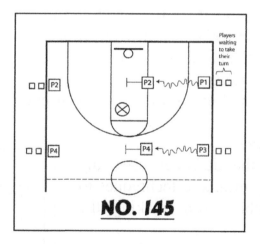

NO. 145

Working the activity:
Have your players line up on both sides of the half court in 2 lines. The front players P1, P3, have the basketball. The players P2, P4, on the other side are the defenders. To start P2, P4 go over and get right in front of P1, P3, about 10 feet away and get into their defensive stance. P1, P3

start a zigzag dribble across the court. P2, P4, have to stay right in front of them while shuffling sideways and moving backwards, and they can't touch P1 or P3. P1, P3, just keep advancing and dribbling while turning a little sideways and dribbling with the backside hand when they get too close. The object is for P2, P4, to stay right in front of P1, P3, while they maintain a 2 or 3 foot distance. For the real little kids you can run the drill only **half way** from center court.

Emphasize: The quick feet, moving backwards, and watching the opponent's stomach area and the ball, they ***DO NOT*** look at the dribblers eyes. They need to get used to doing this.

Run this activity: for about 10 minutes and making sure each player gets at least 2 attempts at guarding the shuffle/slider player all the way across and back. If players are not catching on have an assistant coach pull them aside and show them what they are doing wrong so that the practice does not stop and keeps going.

Skill Activity (No.146) The Guarding the Shooter Drill

Object of the activity: Teach all your players how to guard players dribbling in to the basket to shoot.

What you will need:

You will need half the court, 2 groups of players, 2 basketballs, a coach, and a whistle.

The Basics Are:

In this drill the defender uses any legal guarding means or techniques to stop the dribbler from making the shot.

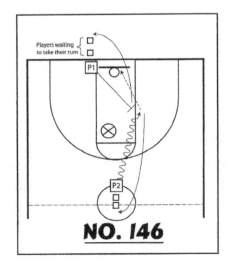

NO. 146

22

Working the activity:
Have your players line up in 2 groups, one at the end of the court under the basket and the other at center court. P1 is the defender and P2 is the shooter with the ball. On the whistle P2 tries to dribble in and make a basket. P1 comes out to stop them. P2 can try a jump shot, or they can try to dribble around P1 and go for a lay-up. P2 can not charge into P1, they have to try and go around. If they run into P1 the drill is dead and they each stop and go to end of the other line. The players should automatically get rotated by changing lines each time the drill is over for them. This drill is run just like a game situation. P1 can't reach in and foul, or the drill stops and both players go back to the end of the line. Blow your whistle on fouls and charging.

Emphasize: Defenders watching only the basketball, they **DO NOT** look at the dribblers eyes. If they are watching the ball they will see the player bring it up when they are going to shoot a jumper. Otherwise they stay right in front of them.

Run this activity: for about 10 minutes and making sure each player gets at least 2 attempts at stopping the shot. If players are not catching on have an assistant coach pull them aside and show them what they are doing wrong so that the practice does not stop and keeps going.

Team Defensive Drills
Explanation
Team defense is probably the most important part of the game. Its defense that wins games. What this means is, stopping the opposing team from scoring points. Each member of the team has a particular job to do when the offense sets up in a certain way. What the offense is doing tells the defense how to set up to defend. "Guards" have a certain way to play, when the opposing team brings the ball in. "Forwards" go to a certain position on the court, when an opposing player is out on the wings, or at the top of the key. "Centers" go to a low post, or a high post, depending on what type of defense the coach wants to play. The basic defenses that are used are the "Man to man", and the "Zone". In the case of "Man to

Man", each player has a particular player to guard, which he stays right on top of, or next to, most of the time.

When a "Zone" defense is played, each player has a particular area of the court to guard, no matter who comes into that area. And some coaches like to use a combination of these defenses in certain cases. We will show you how and what fundamentals to teach at each position.

Skill Activity (No.6) Point Guard Man-To-Man Responsibilities
Object of the activity: Teach all your point guards what their responsibilities are on defense.
What you will need:
You will need half the court, 1 group of point guards, 1 basketball, a coach, and a whistle.
The Basics Are:
When a point guard is playing "Man to Man", there are several responsibilities they have on defense:

1.) Don't let the player they are guarding beat them to the basket on the dribble, stay right between them and the basket at all times.
2.) Always force the player they are guarding, to the outside of the court. Don't let them dribble to the middle of the court if at all possible.
3.) Don't let the player they are guarding shoot a three pointer, without getting their hands up high in front of them to distract them, but don't foul them.

The reason the point guard has these responsibilities is, the opposing guard which they usually guard, will be doing these same kind of things when they come up the court in an attempt to score on offense *(SEE FIGURE 6)*.

24

FIGURE 6

Working the activity:

To practice this play you, or a coach, get a basketball and go out to the mid court line, or out to the sidewalk in front of the garage driveway at home. Then first try to dribble up the middle right to the basket, then the player has to get into their defensive stance *(SEE FIGURE 1).* Next they try to get in front of you in such a way as to force you to go to the outside of the court, or driveway, and away from the basket. If they do manage to get in front of you as you go to the basket, be careful not to knock them down, especially if you are out on the driveway. This is because they will probably get hurt, or skinned up, if they go down on the asphalt.

When they accomplish this technique, then go back and do it again, over and over. You should work on this with them at least 10 or 15 minutes at a time when at home. The *TIP* here is, they must have quick feet in sliding in either direction. And they only watch your (the opponent's) stomach and not their eyes, when they start to move. This way you won't get your feet tangled up, and get faked out by the opponent, when they change directions.

Emphasize:

Defenders watching only the basketball, they **DO NOT** look at the dribblers eyes. If they are watching the ball they will see the player bring it up to shoot a jumper, and react accordingly. Otherwise they stay right in front of the dribbler forcing them outside.

Run this activity: at team practice for about 10 minutes and making sure each player gets at least 2 attempts at stopping the shot. If players are not catching on then you or an assistant coach pull them aside and show them what they are doing wrong so that the practice does not stop and keeps going.

Skill Activity (No.7) Shooting Guard Man-To-Man Responsibilities

Object of the activity: Teach all your shooting guards what their responsibilities are on defense.

What you will need:

You will need half the court, 2 groups of players, one of shooting guards, one of pass catchers, 1 basketball, 2 coaches, and a whistle.

The Basics Are:

When the shooting guard, or "Off Guard" as they are often called, are guarding the other opposing guard without the ball, they have the responsibility of staying right in front of them. This is so they can't catch a pass from the ball handling guard. What they will have to learn how to do is, keep watching the player they are guarding, and out of the corner of their eyes watch the player bringing the ball up the court. This is important for the younger kids because the opponent will pass the ball wildly sometimes without looking, and this lets the off guard intercept the pass.

FIGURE 7

Working the activity:

To practice this play, you will probably need to find another player about the same size to help out. Then you, or a coach, take the basketball and go out to mid court, or out to the sidewalk in front of your garage. Then have your shooting guard go to a spot about 5 feet in front of the basket, and get into their ready stance. Then have your pass catcher get right behind them. Next you start to dribble the ball towards them, and have the pass catcher sneak around them on either side. When the helper gets into the clear, you try to pass them the ball while your shooting guard tries to knock down or catch the pass. Work with them on this for at least 10 or 15 minutes each day, or on the weekend. This will teach them to learn how to stay in front of the opposing player, and not let them catch the pass *(SEE FIGURE 7)*. The <u>*TIP*</u> here is, have quick feet in sliding left or right to stay with the pass catcher.

Emphasize:

To your shooting guards that they keep taking quick glances side to side to see where the pass catcher is so that they don't get fooled where they are.

Run this activity: at team practice for about 10 minutes and making sure each player gets at least 2 attempts at stopping the pass. If players are not catching on then you or an assistant coach pull them aside and show them what they are doing wrong so that the practice does not stop and keeps going.

Skill Activity (No.8) Guards Man-To-Man Rotating

Object of the activity: Teach all your guards how to rotate on covering their assigned player.

What you will need:

You will need half the court, 2 groups of players, one of guards, one of pass catchers, 1 basketball, 2 coaches, and a whistle.

The Basics Are:

This drill is for either "point", or "shooting", guards learning to rotate to help out. I might point out here that for young kids, just starting out at the Atom or Bantam division level, the coaches may not want them to play rotation yet. However, I think your young players still need to know what rotation and switching is, and how it works. Rotating is when a player is guarding an opposing player, man to man, and they leave that player to help out one of their team mates guard an opponent driving in for a shot ***(SEE FIGURE 8)***. This is kind of complicated for little kids because it is a team concept where one of their other team mates has to leave the player they are guarding, and pick up the player they were guarding. It takes a while for a young team to learn this.

FIGURE 8

Working the activity:

To practice this play, you will need to find another player about the same size as your guards, to help you out. Then you, or a coach, take the basketball and go out to mid court or at the sidewalk in front of your garage. Then have your guard, and helper, go to a spot about 5 feet in front of the basket. Next your guard gets in front of the helper, and gets into their defensive "ready stance" *(SEE FIGURE 1)*. Then you, or a coach, start dribbling the ball slowly towards the basket. Have the helper move slowly to their left, with your son or daughter sliding and following them.

When they have moved far enough out the way, to the right of the basket, giving you an open lane to the basket, then you break and dribble fast towards the basket. Try to make a lay-up shot. What they need to do is get in front of you, so you can't make the shot. This is also called "switching off", by some coaches. There is not much room in your driveway, so you might have to walk through this slowly at first until they see how it is done. Then switch, and have them and the helper move to their right (your left), so they get a feel for working on this from the other side of the basket.

They should practice this for at least 10 minutes at a time, if possible. The *TIP* here is, have them learn how to watch you out of the corner of their eye, and break away just as you start to speed up and drive to the basket. This will take some practicing, but don't give up on them because they can learn how to do it. And remember you are bigger than they are, so don't run over them and hurt them on the way to the basket.

Emphasize:

To your guards that they keep taking quick glances side to side to see where the pass catcher and dribbler is so that they can make the quick switch rotation to cover the dribbler.

Run this activity: at team practice for about 10 minutes and making sure each player gets at least 2 attempts at switch rotating. If players are not catching on then you or an assistant coach pull them aside and show them what they are doing wrong so that the practice does not stop and keeps going.

Skill Activity (No.9) Guards Man-To-Man Converging

Object of the activity: Teach all your guards how to converge on a opponent bringing the ball up the court

What you will need:

You will need the full court, two groups of players, one of guards, one of ball dribblers, 1 basketball, 2 coaches, and a whistle.

The Basics Are:

This is a stop the ball handler coming up the court drill (double teaming them). When the opposing guard brings the ball in, and starts to dribble faster up court, both guards suddenly break fast and converge in front of them. Next they get as close as they can without fouling (Touching), put their hands up, wave, and keep the opponent from passing the ball. Usually this will result in a mistake by the ball handler, and causes a turnover (Your team grabs the loose ball). This drill is mostly for "guards", but it won't hurt if "small forwards" learn this also.

FIGURE 9

30

Working the activity:

To practice this play you, or a coach, take the ball and go out to mid court, or the sidewalk, in front of your garage. You will probably need a helper player, about the same size as your guard, to help you on this drill. Have your guard, and the helper go to a spot about 5 feet in front of the basket, and spread out about 10 feet apart. Then you start dribbling the ball fast towards the basket. When your son or daughter, and the helper, see you start to dribble fast, they both quickly break and converge on a spot right in front of you. They both get their hands up while you stop and pretend to pass *(SEE FIGURE 9)*.

Since you are more than likely going to be a lot taller than they are, they probably won't be able to smother you like they would a kid their own size. But they can still get the practice in, on what to do. And they can still try to knock the ball down when you attempt to pass it. They should practice this at least 10 to 15 minutes at a time if possible. If they are making mistakes then stop and correct them. The TIP here is, quick feet and learning how to break quick enough, to allow them time to get in front of the ball handler to cut them off.

Emphasize:

To your guards that they need to break very quickly to converge on the ball handler coming up the court.

Run this activity:

At team practice for about 10 minutes and making sure each player gets at least 2 attempts at converging. If players are not catching on then you or an assistant coach pull them aside and show them what they are doing wrong so that the practice does not stop and keeps going.

Skill Activity (No.10) Small Forward Man-To-Man Responsibilities

Object of the activity: Teach all your small forwards what their responsibilities are on defense.

What you will need:

You will need half the court, 2 groups of players, one of small forwards, one of pass catchers, 1 basketball, 2 coaches, and a whistle.

The Basics Are:

The "small forwards" job, in the man to man defense is a little more simpler than a guard. They have to basically keep passes from getting in to the low post player they are guarding. If the small forward lets the ball handler pass the ball, in to the player they are guarding in the low post area, he probably will score a basket most of the time. Also they need to seal off the player they are guarding, from dribble driving the basket. They have to learn how to steal any passes to the player they are guarding when that player attempts to cut around in back of them for a lay-up.

Step 1   **FIGURE 10**   Step 2

Working the activity:

To practice this play you, or a coach, take the ball and go to the mid court line, or out to the sidewalk in front of your garage. You will need another player, about the same size as your small forward to help you out. Send your small forward to a spot way out on the wing area, to the right side of the basket. Have the pass catcher get in front of them, then you start to dribble towards the them, then have the pass catcher cut around to their left, behind your small forward towards the basket. Then you attempt to pass the ball to the pass catcher. Your small forward then has to whirl

32

around to their left, raise their right hand, slide step, then stay between the helper and you. Then your small forward has to look back at you, and attempt to knock down the pass, or catch the ball (*SEE FIGURE 10*). To make this play work for them, they will have to learn to keep quickly turning their head back and forth to watch you, then watch the pass catcher.

If the player they are guarding does get the pass, and takes a short jump shot, then your small forward has to remember to whirl around, and box them out from getting to any rebound (*SEE FIGURE 4*). After you practice this over on the right side, then move over to the left side and flip flop or reverse everything. They need to learn how to make this play, on either the left or right wing area of the court. They should practice this at least 10 minutes at a time, if possible.

If they are making mistakes, like on whirling, then stop and correct their mistakes by walking them through this slowly. The *TIP* here is, quick feet, and the cross over foot whirl. This is why doing all that practice with the crossover foot agility drill comes in handy. If they whirl the wrong way they will sometimes get their feet tangled up, trip, and fall down. Leaving the player they were guarding wide open to go to the basket for a lay-up.

Emphasize:
To your small forwards that they need to learn how to whirl around quickly without getting their feet tangled up.

Run this activity:
At team practice for about 10 minutes and making sure each small forward gets at least 2 attempts at blocking the play. If players are not catching on then you or an assistant coach pull them aside and show them what they are doing wrong so that the practice does not stop and keeps going.

Skill Activity (No.11, 12) Power Forward Man-To-Man Responsibilities

Object of the activity: Teach all your power forwards what their responsibilities are on defense.

What you will need:

You will need half the court, 2 groups of players, one of power forwards, one of pass catchers, 1 basketball, 2 coaches, and a whistle.

The Basics Are:

The" power forwards" job, in the man to man defense is also a little more simpler than a guards responsibilities. They have to basically keep passes from getting in to the low post player they are guarding. If the power forward lets the ball handler pass the ball in to the player they are guarding, in the low post area, they probably will score a basket most of the time. When they are in the low post area, they need to seal off opposing players attempting to drive to the basket. They have to learn how to steal, or knock down, passes to players attempting to cut around, or behind, them for a lay-up. And if they get right in front of, and between the player and the basket, just let the player run into them and take a charging foul. If they are bigger than the player cutting to the basket, this should not be a problem. Tell them to just use their strength, to hold their seal off position.

Working the activity:

To practice this drill you, or a coach, take the ball and go to the mid court line or out to the sidewalk in front of your garage. You will need another player, about the same size as your power forward, to help you out. Send your power forward to a spot about 5 feet out from the basket, and to the right side. Have the helper player get in front of them, then you start to dribble, then have the pass catcher cut around to the left, and behind your power forward, towards the basket. Then you attempt to pass them the ball. Your power forward then has to whirl around to their left, raise their right hand, slide step, then stay between the helper and you. Then your power forward has to look back at you, and attempt to knock down the pass, or catch the ball *(SEE FIGURE 11)*. To make this play work for them, they will have to learn to keep quickly turning their head, back and forth to watch you then watch the pass catcher. Sometimes pass the ball to the pass catcher, then have your power forward slide in front of the helper, attempting to drive to the basket, seal them off, and take a "charging foul" *(SEE FIGURE 12)*. To get the foul called though, remember to explain to them that they have to already be in position directly in front of the player breaking for the basket, and between that player and the basket.

FIGURE 11

FIGURE 12

If the player they are guarding does manage to get the pass, and takes a short jump shot, then remember to teach them to whirl around, and box the player out from getting to any rebound *(SEE FIGURE 4)*. After you practice this over on the RIGHT side, then move over to the LEFT side and practice, by flip flopping and reversing the moves. They need to learn how to make this play, on either the left or right, at the low post area of the court. They should practice this at least 10 minutes at a time, if possible. If they are making mistakes, like on whirling, then stop and correct their mistakes by walking them through this slowly. The *TIP* here is, quick feet, and the cross over foot whirl. This is where doing all that

35

practice with the crossover foot agility drill comes in handy. If they whirl the wrong way, they will sometimes get their feet tangled up, trip, and fall down. This leaves the player they were guarding wide open, to go to the basket for a lay-up.

Emphasize:

To your power forwards that they need to learn how to whirl around quickly without getting their feet tangled up.

Run this activity:

At team practice for about 10 minutes and making sure each power forward gets at least 3 attempts at converging. If players are not catching on then you or an assistant coach pull them aside and show them what they are doing wrong so that the practice does not stop and keeps going.

Skill Activity (No.13, 14) Center Man-To-Man Responsibilities

Object of the activity: Teach all your centers what their responsibilities are on defense.

What you will need:

You will need half the court, 2 groups of players, one of centers, one of dribbler/shooters, 1 basketball, 2 coaches, and a whistle.

The Basics Are:

The main job of the center is, stop opposing players from driving to the basket for lay-ups, box out after they shoot, and grab all rebounds. They are usually the tallest, and the biggest, player on the court. But because they are so tall and big, they are not always too coordinated. So they have to work hard to learn all the basic fundamentals. Here are the basics they need to learn:

1.) After a player releases their shot, they have to whirl around and box out.

2.) When they are guarding, or going out to try and block an opposing players shot, they need to get both arms straight up to obstruct that players view of the basket, or to block the shot.

3.) .They have to learn to not react to an opposing players faking with the ball.

4.) .They need to learn to keep their hand lightly on the opposing centers back, but not lean up against him, and get a foul called against them.

5) .They have to learn to anticipate where the player they are guarding wants to go, then when that player starts their move, your son or daughter needs to beat them to that spot.

6.) .Don't play in front of the player they are guarding because the ball handler may make a lob pass over their head, and let that player make a basket.

7) They have to learn how to block shots, by getting a hand on the ball and deflecting it.

8) Also along with this, they need to learn to not touch the player's arms or body but just the ball.

FIGURE 13

FIGURE 14

Working the activity:

To practice these plays, have your center go out to a spot about 5 feet in front of the basket. Then you, or a coach, take the basketball and go out to spot about 8 feet in front of them. Next start your dribble right to the basket, and try to make a lay-up shot. Their job is, come out, and get right in front of you and block your path to the basket, and take a charging foul if you run into them *(SEE FIGURE 12)*. You may want to practice this in slow motion, so no one gets hurt accidentally. Work on this play about 3 or 4 times. Then on the next time stop short of dribbling just in front of them jump up and try to shoot a short jump shot. Their reaction should be to come right in front of you when they see you are going to shoot, instead of dribbling by them. They should jump up with both hands straight up in air, in front of your view of the basket *(SEE FIGURE 13)*. Work on this play 3 or 4 times.

Now they are not sure when you are going to change again, so then you dribble right at them. Then when you get close to them, give them a head fake, try to sneak around them on the other side, away from the fake side. Do this for about 3 or 4 times. For this next practice exercise, you will need a helper player to help you. Have your center stay in the same starting place, then put the helper behind them under the basket. Then you start your dribble right at them, but when you start to get close, you lob the ball over their head to the helper. This has to done quickly before your center can get their hands up. After a few times, they will see when you are going to lob the ball, then they should stop, jump up with one or both hands straight up in the air, and try to catch the lob. Do this 3 or 4 times.

On this practice exercise, both of you go back to the same places, start your dribble right at them, and tell them they have to try to block the shot this time. Then start your dribble, and when they come up to block your path, stop and try to make a short jump shot over the top of them. Since they are practicing the block, have them watch the ball and nothing else when they come up to make the block *(SEE FIGURE 14)*. Observe and make sure they get one or both hands on the ball, and not hit you or your arm for a foul. And since you are probably much taller than they are, make it fair and don't jump up for the shot. Do this for about 3 or 4 times.

For this practice exercise, have them go to their starting spot again. Then you, or a coach, get right in front of them, with your back to them. This is a another type of drill for shot blocking. Then when you are ready, whirl around to either side of them, and try to shoot a jump shot. What they should do is put their hand lightly on your back, to keep their space, until they see what you are going to do *(SEE FIGURE 5)*. When they see that you are going to whirl around to the side of them, they drop their hand on your back then slide over to the same side you turn to. Next they put their hands up, to make it harder for you to see the basket, or they try to block the shot *(SEE FIGURE 13)*. Make sure they don't touch you or your arm for a foul. If they touch the ball though, its ok. All they need to do is touch enough of the ball to deflect it, not try to slap it way into the next county. Do this for about 3 or 4 times.

For this practice exercise, both of you take the same positions as before with you right in front of them, with your back to them. This is a drill for "boxing out" and rebounding. Then when you are ready, whirl around to either side, and make a jump shot to the basket. Their reaction should be to try to block your view or the shot *(SEE FIGURE 13)*. If you do manage to get the shot off on its way to the basket, their reaction should be to whirl around and box you out from trying to go to the basket to grab the rebound *(SEE FIGURE 4)*. The _TIP_ here for all these drills is, do a lot of work with your players on the coordination drills, so they develop quick feet.

Emphasize:
To your centers that they need to keep their hands up, and stay right in front of the dribbler shooter.

Run this activity:
At team practice for about 10 minutes and making sure each center gets at least 4 attempts at blocking the play. If players are not catching on then you or an assistant coach pull them aside and show them what they are doing wrong so that the practice does not stop and keeps going.

Skill Activity (No.15) Man-To-Man Screen Responsibilities
Object of the activity: Teach all your players how to deal with screens and what their responsibilities are on defense.
What you will need:
You will need half the court, 2 groups of players, one of defenders, one of screeners/dribblers, 1 basketball, 2 coaches, and a whistle.

The Basics Are:
This drill is for all players, but mostly for guards and forwards. Screens are when a player is guarding the opponent, they are assigned to guard, and that player uses one of his own team mates as a blocker. This is to get rid of your player guarding them, so they can get open for a pass or a shot. What happens is the ball handler maneuvers around, so his team mate (usually a big center or power forward) can slide in between the two of you. Then they stand there flat footed and still. Then just when the blocker gets between you, the player breaks in another direction, then they move to an open spot to catch a pass, or get a jump shot off to the basket.

Of course when you try to slide with them, you run into this big player blocking you (the screener) from staying with the player you are guarding. The defensive player being screened has two choices. They can try to go around the blocker, and stay with their man, or they can yell "SWITCH", and stay guarding the blocker. When they yell switch, one of their nearby team mates picks up and guards the opposing player, who slipped around the screen. The danger with the switch is, if you are a small guard, you may end up trying to guard a bigger player, who may get the ball then over power you to the basket for a shot. Also this
40

concept will only work if the players on your team have been taught how to "SWITCH" correctly. If they have *not* been taught, your players will have to keep practicing on how to get around the screen, then it is a must that they maintain contact with the player they were guarding.

FIGURE 15

Working the activity:

What you can do to practice this play is, teach them both ways. And they will have to learn to analyze the situation, to determine which technique to use if they are *"Screened"*. First you, or a coach, take the ball and go out to mid court, or out to the sidewalk in front of the garage. At this point you will need a helper, who will act as the blocker. Have your player go to a spot about 5 feet out in front of the basket. Have the helper get just to their left, and next to them. Then you start your dribble right at your defender. When you start to get close to them, you *fake* going around to the left side of them. Next the helper will have to get right up close to them, and when the helper can see that you are getting close, they just stop. Then you switch and go around to the right of them, for a lay-up to the basket. And at that point the helper has to get right off their left front shoulder, and stay in contact with them to act as a blocker between you and your defender *(SEE FIGURE 15)*. At that point have the defender yell "SWITCH", and move around quickly in front of the blocker and start guarding them. And just for your information, when the blocker does this for the ball handler, it is called a "Pick and Roll" play. The "Roll" comes from having the blocker roll back towards the basket after the switch, then the ball handler passes back to him for the lay up. Work on this play for at least 4 or 5 times every practice until they are beginning to get the idea of how it feels when they get blocked. Remember to explain to your defender that if at all possible, be ready for the screen and fight through it, to stay with the player they are guarding. They only do a switch when they see that there is no way they can get around the screen.

For the next practice exercise you, and your defender, go back to the same starting positions, except this time the helper stands to the right side of them. All of you do the same things as before, except this time when you make your change of direction to the left, the blocker just stands there leaving room for your defender to go around behind them (to let then make a play on you). Your son or daughter then goes right around behind them, and keeps sliding to their right, guarding you from getting to the basket for the lay-up. Do this play about 4 or 5 times every practice. The *TIP* here is have them work on their quick footwork and learning how to tell when to fight through the screen, or stay there for the switch and guard.

Emphasize:
To your players that they need to learn when to switch and when to go around the screener. This is not always an easy decision it just takes a lot of practice to learn how to make the right decision.

Run this activity:
At team practice for about 10 minutes and making sure each player gets at least 2 attempts as the defender. Don't forget to rotate your screeners and dribblers so that they get a chance to be the defender. If players are not catching on then you or an assistant coach pull them aside and show

them what they are doing wrong so that the practice does not stop and keeps going.

Skill Activity (No.16, 17) General Shot Blocking

Object of the activity: Teach all your players the basics for shot blocking

What you will need:

You will need half the court, 2 groups of players, one of shot blockers, one of pass shooters, 1 basketball, 2 coaches, and a whistle.

The Basics Are:

All players need to learn the basics of shot blocking on defense. However, the two players that need to really work on learning this technique are "centers," and "power forwards." This is because they are usually the tallest players on the team, and they have the longest arms. To get the blocked shot called fair though, the ball has to be on the way _up_ to the basket, and _not_ after it starts back down on its trajectory. If they swat (block) it on its trajectory down to the basket, its ruled as "goal tending", the basket then counts.

So, the best way to make a block is, get your hand on it just as the ball handler starts the shot, or the pass *(SEE FIGURE 17)*. At this point explain to your son or daughter that in order to practice the shot block they need to focus in on the ball, as they get close to the ball handler, then never take their eyes off the ball. To learn how to do this will just take a lot of practice, over and over. If you can teach them to make blocks, they will go far in basketball, especially if they are big and tall

Working the activity:

To practice these techniques, have your defender go to a spot out about 5 feet in front of the basket. Next you, or a coach, get about 10 feet out in front of them, so you have space to dribble the ball. Dribble straight at them, and first try to stop just in front of them, and shoot a short jump shot. What they should do is, come right up close to you and focus on the ball. Then just as the ball bounces down and starts to come up, they reach out, focus on the ball with their eyes, then with the palm of their hand facing forward, push it right at the ball *(SEE FIGURE 16),* deflecting it away. Do at least about 5 or 6 of these plays at every practice.

FIGURE 16

FIGURE 17

If they are not catching on how to do this, then you might try this out to quicken their hands. Stand right in front of them, hold the ball tightly in front of your chest *(SEE FIGURE 17).* Then have them stand about 2 or 3 feet in front of you. Hold tight on the ball and holler "Reach". When they hear that, they lunge out with their hand and hit the ball as fast as they can, with the palm facing forward and fingers up. They need to bring the hand back quickly though so they don't foul the opponent. Then react to whether they made the block or not. The other way to attempt to make a block is, watch the ball handlers free hand. Then when they get close to you, the free hand will move around to grab the ball to steady it for a pass or a shot, then have your son or daughter quickly switch their focus to the ball, and reach for the block *(SEE FIGURE 17).* Do at least about 5 or 6 of these plays at every practice. The <u>*TIP*</u> here is, teach them to have quick hands, focus, keep their eyes on the ball, and don't look at <u>*opponents eyes*</u> when they get close, all of this as they are about to make their reach.

44

Emphasize:

To your players that they need to learn how to watch the ball and NOT the opponent's eyes.

Run this activity:

At team practice for about 10 minutes and making sure each player forward gets at least 3 attempts at blocking a shot. If players are not catching on then you or an assistant coach pull them aside and show them what they are doing wrong so that the practice does not stop and keeps going.

Skill Activity (No.18, 19) General Making Steals

Object of the activity: Teach all your players the basics for making steals.

What you will need:

You will need half the court, 2 groups of players, one of shot blockers, one of pass shooters, 1 basketball, 2 coaches, and a whistle.

The Basics Are:

All players need to learn the basic fundamentals of making steals. But mostly "guards" and "small forwards" need to learn this technique. All of the following are qualified as a steal:

1.) Grabbing the ball away from an opposing player, without fouling them.

2.) Making a "Held ball" play, and causing the ball to go over to your team on a possession.

3.) Intercepting an opposing players pass, and gaining control of the ball.

4.) Batting the ball off an opposing player, who is standing in bounds, and having it go out of bounds, giving your team the possession.

FIGURE 18

FIGURE 19

5.) Batting the ball off an opposing player, and having it deflected to a player on your team.

Working the activity:

To practice making steals, first have your players go to a spot out about 12 feet in front of the basket. Then you, or a coach, will need to get a helper player. Have the helper stand about 5 or 6 feet behind them. Then you, or a coach, go out to mid court or out on the sidewalk in front of the garage. Then slowly start to dribble right at your defender. After a couple of dribbles attempt to pass the ball to the helper player. Explain to the helper that they have to start out right behind your defender, then they can move to either side while your defender watches you. When they are clear to the either side, then you stop, and pass the ball to the helper player. Your defender has to watch you and the helper, by glancing back and forth, and when you pass the ball they attempt to catch it. Do this about 4 or 5 times each practice.

For the second practice, you stand about 6 feet in front of your defender, and slowly start to dribble the ball towards them. When you get close, give them a head fake, start dribbling faster, and try to go around either side of them. And when you get close, they need to start focusing on the

46

ball, and attempt to grab it away from you. And they have to accomplish the steal without touching you for a foul. This is very hard to learn, without fouling the opponent. Teach them to have quick hands. They will only learn this by practicing it, over and over. Do this at least about 4 or 5 times each practice.

For the third practice, both of you go back to the starting position. Start dribbling the ball right towards them, then just like the second drill, make your move to go around them. Except this time have your defender just grab the ball with both hands, and hold on for a *"Held Ball"*. Their move should be to just watch the ball when you get close, then grab it and hold on. Teach them to make their move just as the dribbler starts to push the ball down. Make sure you keep dribbling, but let them grab it some of the time. Do this at least 4 or 5 times each practice.

For the fourth practice, have your defender stand right near a base line or a side line. Pick a spot where there is room for them to jump up in the air out of bounds. Then you, or a coach, take the ball and stand about 3 or 4 feet away from them. Next you lob the ball up in the air, just slightly out of bounds. Have them jump up in the air, out of bounds, and swat (bat) the ball while it is still in the air, right back at you. While in the air they need to take aim at your lower legs, which is where they want to swat the ball *(SEE FIGURE 18)*. The ball should hit your lower legs then bounce out of bounds. Explain to them that if they swat it up higher, you may be able to catch it, and it won't go out of bounds. They will need to practice this play a lot because it is very hard to learn especially for 5 to 7 year olds. You may want to wait until they get older, to practice this technique with them. Do this at least about 4 or 5 times each practice.

For the fifth practice, both of you go back to the starting positions on the forth practice. You will need a helper player again for this technique. Have the helper go to an inbounds spot about 6 feet away from you. To start the play you, or a coach, lob the ball up in the air. Except lob it inbounds, slightly away from your defender. What your defender has to do is, jump up as they go out of bounds, and swat (bat) the ball off your legs so that it goes directly to the helper *(SEE FIGURE 19)*. The ball should bounce off your lower legs, down low, where you can't catch it. Something to point out here, since you know what they are trying to do don't reach down and catch it. Just stand there and see where it hits on your legs. This will be very hard for them to learn. If they can't seem to get it to deflect off of you to the helper, don't worry about it. Most of the time the situation where they would need to do this will never come up. However it is a legitimate steal play, and they need to at least know how it works. So make sure they know how to at least attempt it. Do this at least about 5 or 6 times, at maybe two practices, so they will remember. The *TIP* here is, work on their quick hands and feet, and have them work on keeping their eyes only on the ball.

Emphasize:
To your players that they need to learn how to watch the ball and NOT the opponent's eyes.

Run this activity:
At team practice for about 10 minutes and making sure each player gets at least 2 attempts at making this steal attempt play. If players are not catching on then you or an assistant coach pull them aside and show them what they are doing wrong so that the practice does not stop and keeps going.

Skill Activity (No.20, 21) Man-To-Man Rebounding
Object of the activity: Teach all your players how to deal with rebounding and what their responsibilities are on defense.

What you will need:
You will need half the court, 2 groups of players, one of defenders, one of helpers, 1 basketball, 2 coaches, and a whistle.

The Basics Are:
All players should learn the techniques of rebounding. But mostly "centers", and "power forwards," need to really work on this technique. This is where those drills on jumping come in handy. They have to get strength in their legs, to be able to get way up in the air for rebounds.

Many times your tall defender may not be too athletic, with respect to their jumping abilities. I have watched many young boys and girls, who are centers, just stand flat footed under the basket, and wait for the ball to come down to them. Tell that If the coach puts them under the basket on defense, it's probably because they want them to get most of the rebounds. If your under the basket players have these problems, you will probably need to light a fire under them to make them aggressive.

Teach them to be aware of where the ball might go when a shot is made. To get the rebound they have to be in the right spot, or it might come down on the opposite side of basket from where they are standing. And once they get to the right spot, you need to teach them to "box out" the player they are guarding, or any opposing player in that spot. Teach your defenders that actually rebounding is their job on defense, no matter what position they play. In a "man to man" defense, if all your players keep the opposing player they are guarding from getting a rebound, they have done a good job.

FIGURE 20

FIGURE 21

Working the activity:

To practice rebounding you, or a coach, take the ball out to a spot about 14 or 15 feet out in front of the basket, or by the sidewalk in front of the garage. You will need a helper player to work on this play with you Have your defender go out to a spot about 5 feet in front of the basket. Have the helper go to a spot about 4 or 5 feet away from your defender. Then you, or a coach, shoot the ball at the basket. Try to make your shot miss going in the basket, and bounce off the rim in some way. When they see you make your shot, both your defender and the helper need to turn, face the basket, and attempt to grab the rebound. If your defender can see that the rebound might go towards the helpers area, they need to slide over in front of the helper and "box them out" of position, by getting between them and the basket *(SEE FIGURE 4).*

And point out to your defender that when they "box out," they have to keep pushing backwards, maintaining contact with the player they are boxing out. Also tell them to not be afraid to use their behind (no hands though), to push with, and maintain contact with the opponent. Then when the ball starts to come down, they jump way up in the air to grab it away from the helper *SEE FIGURE 20).* When they go up in the air on the left side of the basket, they should reach up with their left hand, and bend the free hand at the elbow, to keep other players away from the ball. And when they go up on the right side of the basket , they should reach up with the right hand.

As soon as they make contact with the ball on their finger tips, they need to quickly bring the other hand up, grab the ball with both hands around it, then come back down so that the helper can't reach over and knock the ball loose *(SEE FIGURE 21).* Work on this play at least 5 or 6 times each practice. The *TIP* here is, make sure they use their behind to push way back, help them learn how to judge when to jump up, and then make sure they do.

Emphasize:

To your players that they need to learn to be good at boxing out then just at the right time jumping way up in the air to get the rebound.

Run this activity:

At team practice for about 10 minutes and making sure each player gets at least 2 attempts at rebounding. Don't forget to rotate your helper so that they get a chance to be the defender. If players are not catching on then you or an assistant coach pull them aside and show them what they are doing wrong so that the practice does not stop and keeps going.

Skill Activity (No.22) General Diving for Loose Balls

Object of the activity: Teach all your players how to dive and recover loose balls.

What you will need:

You will need a corner on the court, 1 group of players, preferably a landing mat, 1 basketball, 1 coach, and a whistle.

The Basics Are:

Not every coach wants to teach this skill, but believe me it is an important part of the game. All players need to learn how to do this. U.C.L.A.'s John Wooden stressed this to his players all the time. What this is mainly for is, learn how to get to loose balls, and gain possession.

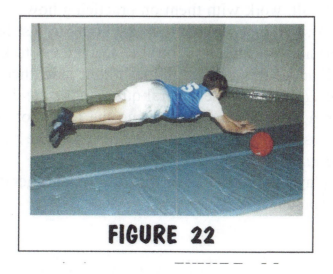

FIGURE 22

Working the activity:

For practicing this technique, you better go out to the back yard, or the park someplace where there is thick grass. Or if you are in the gym ask if you can borrow one of their mats. Also if you can afford it, get them some knee pads for this drill, so they don't hurt their knees while practicing. To practice this play you, or a coach, take the ball and go out about 10 feet in front of them. Have your son or daughter get into their "ready stance" *(SEE FIGURE 3)*. Next you roll the ball slowly, at a spot about 5 feet to the side of them. First to the right of them then to the left of them.

What your players have to do is, watch the ball with their eyes focused on it, turn, and dive out in the air to intercept the ball *(SEE FIGURE 22)*. Once they do get their hands on the ball, they need to cover it up with both hands so that an opposing player does not come up and grab or knock it away. Teach them to be aware of where the nearest opposing player is. If no opposing player is close, then they can quickly get straight up and to their feet. But if an opposing player is right next to them, they can roll away in the opposite direction, and scramble to their feet.

If they just lay there with the ball, an opposing player can come up and grab onto the ball for a *"Held Ball"*. And that could be a turnover if the possession arrow is in favor of the other team. So once they learn how to get to the ball, work with them on practicing how to get up quickly with the ball. Also if they see that they are going to just barely reach the ball, but not be able to catch or control it, teach them to knock it away out of bounds. Practice this at least 5 times to one side, then 5 times to the other side. The _TIP_ here is, use several quick foot steps in the direction of the ball, then a push off and dive, using the lead foot as the push off foot. Also make sure they always keep their eyes on the ball.

Emphasize:

To your players that they need to learn to get a good push off then keep their eyes on the ball.

Run this activity:

At team practice for about 10 minutes and making sure each player gets at least 2 attempts as the diving for the ball. If players are not catching on then you or an assistant coach pull them aside and show them what they are doing wrong so that the practice does not stop and keeps going.

Skill Activity (No.23) Guards in a 2-3 Zone Defense

Object of the activity: Teach all your guards how to guard opponents while in a 2-3 zone defense.

What you will need:

You will need half the court, 1 group of guards, 1 group of helpers 1 basketball, 1 coach, and a whistle.

The Basics Are:

In a simple common zone such as a 2-3 zone, both guards have the responsibility to guard the perimeter wing areas. One guard has an area on one side, from the free throw line out to the wing perimeter on that side. The other guard takes the same area on the opposite side. The problem with this defense is, the opposing team might have 3 good outside shooters. What that does is, it leaves 2 guards that have to guard 3 players from taking an easy jumper, or a 3 point shot. And that usually makes for a big mismatch. In the zone though, if those players do get by the guards and into the lane, they are no longer the responsibility of either guard. The center, or a forward, has to pick them up.

When the ball handler is out in the wing area, another player has to slide over and help guard the opposing center, by getting in front of them. This is to keep them from getting a pass from the ball handler. This would be one of the forwards. In this 2-3 zone the guards also have the responsibility to keep the ball handler from dribbling in between them, to the basket, or making a short jump shot. They have to also stop any one of the 3 players, from penetrating the perimeter. Tell them that playing in a zone defense, they should always get their hands up to deflect passes from the opposing players because they are probably not playing real close to them, like in a man to man defense.

53

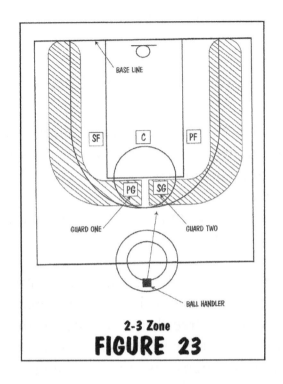

BASE LINE

SF   C   PF

PG   SG

GUARD ONE   GUARD TWO

BALL HANDLER

2-3 Zone
FIGURE 23

Working the activity:

To practice this play, have your defender go to a spot out about 15 to 18 feet in front of the basket (About at the free throw line) **SEE FIGURE 23.** You will need a helper to work on this play. Then take the ball and you and the helper go out to mid court, or out on the sidewalk in front of the garage. Next you start dribbling the ball right at your defender, and have the helper move right along parallel with you, but on the wing. When you get close to your defender player, try to dribble around them. Other times try passing over to the helper, then the helper tries to dribble around them. What you have to teach your defender is, to slide in front of you and block your path. Then the minute you pass over to the helper, they have to rotate (slide) over towards the other part of the court, but within their zone area only. What this teaches them to do is rotate, and follow. Look at the diagram for 2-3 zone defense, and point out to them which basic area they have to defend *(SEE FIGURE 23),* instead of

guarding man to man style. What they basically have to learn is to rotate around, and face, the opposing players as they come down court into their zone. I wouldn't practice this too much with the 5 to 7 year old kids just enough so they understand how it works. When they get on their first team, or your team, then you can decide which type of defense you want to run. Usually coaches don't try to teach a zone defense until young kids have been playing a few years. The *TIP* here is as the opposing guards start to get near your defenders
zone, they need to get their hands up, and rotate slightly towards the side the ball handler is on.

Emphasize:
To your players that they need to learn how to get their hands up and rotate towards the ball.

Run this activity:
At team practice for about 10 minutes and making sure each guard gets at least 2 attempts at playing in their zone. If players are not catching on then you or an assistant coach pull them aside and show them what they are doing wrong so that the practice does not stop and keeps going.

Skill Activity (No.24) Forwards in a 2-3 Zone Defense
Object of the activity: Teach all your forwards how to guard opponents while in a 2-3 zone defense.

What you will need:
You will need half the court, 1 group of forwards, 1 group of helpers 1 basketball, 1 coach, and a whistle.

The Basics Are:
In the 2-3 zone, the forwards have to guard the wing areas until their guards get up into their locations, then they go back to their own zone area, and guard that side of the basket. What forwards basically do is, kind of form a line with the center, to keep the opposing players from getting through the line and sneaking in behind them, under the basket for an easy shot. They need to make sure that no opposing player gets around them on the base line *(SEE FIGURE 24).* If they can force the

opposing players to go around them, towards the middle of the court, they will get more help there from their team mates. If an opposing player moves right to the base line, they need to guard them very tightly, so they can not catch a pass for an easy basket.

Working the activity:

To practice this play you will need one or two helpers. Then you, or a coach, take the ball and go out to mid court, or out on the sidewalk in front of the garage. Next have your forwards go to their area on the right and left side of the basket. Then you start dribbling the ball right at your defender, and the helper moves right along with you, but parallel along the right side of the court. Then suddenly have the helper break for a spot right on the base line, and on the edge of the line for the right side of the lane (The low post area). As your defender sees the helper break for that spot, behind them on the base line, they have to block the helpers path and force them into the lane area in front of them where the center is ***(SEE Page 8 & FIGURE 24).***

While doing all of this, make sure they stay in their zone area. Again practice this a few times with them, to make sure they understand what to do. But don't spend a lot of time on it until they start playing a zone defense. I have watched some of the young 7 and 8 year old teams play, and I could not tell what defense they were using. If you don't know, don't be afraid to ask the coach, are they playing a zone defense. The *TIP* here is, make sure they get their hands up when an opposing player heads into their zone. And make sure they seal off (Keep them from catching a pass) any opposing players that try to get to, or camp under, the basket in the low post area ***(SEE PAGE 8).***

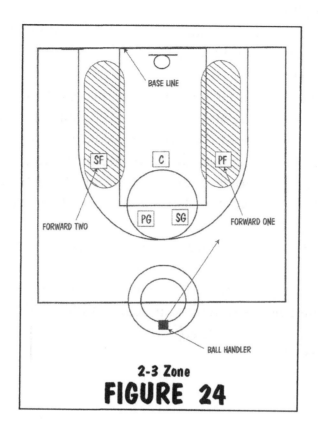

2-3 Zone

FIGURE 24

Emphasize:

To your players that they need to learn how to get their hands up and rotate towards the ball.

Run this activity:

At team practice for about 10 minutes and making sure each forward gets at least 2 attempts at playing in their zone. If players are not catching on then you or an assistant coach pull them aside and show them what they are doing wrong so that the practice does not stop and keeps going.

Skill Activity (No.25) Centers in a 2-3 Zone Defense

Object of the activity: Teach all your centers how to guard opponents while in a 2-3 zone defense.

What you will need:

You will need half the court, 1 group of centers, 1 group of helpers 1 basketball, 1 coach, and a whistle.

The Basics Are:

In a 2-3 zone, the center has to guard the paint in the center of the lane, and the low post areas on either side of the basket. The center forms kind of a blocking line, with the two forwards. If an opposing player tries to drive to the basket, up the middle of the lane, from the wings or the base line, the center has to seal them off (Keep them from breaking through) *SEE PAGE 8*. The center also has to seal off any opposing players that break through the forwards, and down the base line. The center always has help around the post area, in a zone defense, with a forward on each side. However, it is still their main job to box out and rebound, if an opposing player does get off a shot at the basket *(SEE FIGURE 3)*. The area the center needs to defend is really quite small, compared to the area a guard has to cover *(SEE FIGURE 23, 25)*.

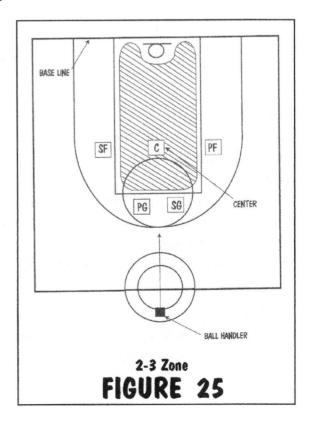

2-3 Zone
FIGURE 25

Working the activity:
To practice this play you will need one or two helpers. Then you, or a coach, go out to mid court, or on the sidewalk in front of the garage. Next have your center go to their area in front of the basket. Then you start dribbling the ball right at them, and the helper moves right along with you, but parallel along the right side of the court. When you get close to your center, attempt to drive around them right to the basket. The centers job is to get in front of you, and take a ***"charging foul"*** if necessary, but keep you from getting around them for a basket.

Practice this a few times, then the next time you dribble at them, pass the ball to the helper over on the right side, just before you get to them. The helper goes way out in the wing area, and on the base line, and waits for your pass ***(SEE PAGE 8)***. When the helper gets your pass, they try to dribble drive right down the base line to the basket. What your center needs to do is, just as they see you pass the ball way over to the helper, swing around quickly, and move over to the low post area on the right side of the basket.

And what they have to do when they get there is, get in position to seal off before the helper can dribble to the basket, for a lay-up shot. Again as I said before work on this play a few times, but don't spend a lot of time on it until your son or daughter gets on a team using a zone defense. The _TIP_ here is when they see the opposing team start to come up the court, they get their hands up to deflect any quick passes. And have them work on their quickness of feet, in turning, and pivoting , to move to the seal off spot.

Emphasize:
To your players that they need to learn how to get their hands up and rotate towards the ball.

Run this activity:
At team practice for about 10 minutes and making sure each center gets at least 2 attempts at playing in their zone. If players are not catching on

then you or an assistant coach pull them aside and show them what they are doing wrong so that the practice does not stop and keeps going.

Skill Activity (No.26) Rebounding and Steals in a Zone Defense

Object of the activity: Teach all your players how to rebound and steal while in a zone defense.

What you will need:
You will need half the court, 1 group of players, 1 group of helpers 1 basketball, 1 coach, and a whistle.

The Basics Are:
Use the same drills as in the man to man defense section of the book *(SEE SKILL ACTIVITY 18 TO 21).* There is no difference in either man to man, or zone defenses, for improving on these skills.

Working the activity:
For steals and rebounding in a zone defense, the practice would be the same as in *SKILL ACTIVITY 18 TO 21,* for "man to man".

Skill Activity (No.27, 28, 29) Other Zone Defenses

Object of the activity:
Teach all your players how to guard opponents while in other zone defenses.

What you will need:
You will need half the court, 1 group of players, 1 group of helpers 1 basketball, 1 coach, and a whistle.

The Basics Are:
So far we have shown the 2-3 zone defense, mostly because it is one of the more popular zone defenses. However, there are many other zone type defenses. One of the other more popular zone defenses is the 1-3-1 *(SEE FIGURE 27).* This defense is designed to force the opposing team to take long corner shots. It also makes it harder for the opposing team to get rebounds.

1-3-1 Zone
FIGURE 27

There is a "Triangle and Two" type of zone defense *(SEE FIGURE 28)*. This defense is designed to have the three triangle players in the paint *(SEE PAGE 8)*, play a zone defense, and keep any player from penetrating to the basket. The other two players rotate around, play man to man, and keep pressure on the ball handlers. So actually this is a combination defense, not a full zone type defense.

Another defense that is common is the "Box and One". This defense is designed to stop the other team when they have one big dominant, tall, player. The four players in the box play a zone defense. The other player tightly guards the dominant player where ever they go, and keep a constant pressure on them. *(SEE FIGURE 29)*. The player, that guards the dominant player, has to have a lot of endurance because they will have to chase that player all over the court, most of the game. And they will have to be a very good defensive player, to stay out of foul trouble.

This is also a combination defense. The best defensive guard, or forward on the team, needs to play up in the front of the Box, to also help keep the dominant player from penetrating the Box Zone area of the paint *(SEE PAGE 8).* This strategy could work against a youth team that has maybe only one good, tall, player on their team.

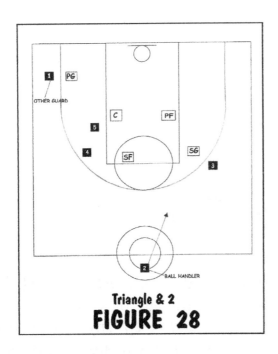

Triangle & 2
FIGURE 28

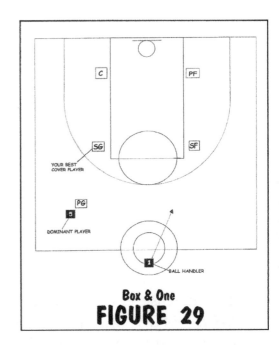

Box & One
FIGURE 29

Working the activity:
If your defender is on a team using any of these defenses, you can go back then and practice with them on these drills. Because basically in any *"Zone"* defense, they just rotate around in their area, and seal off. And basically in a *"Man to Man"* defense, they have to stay right with the player they are guarding wherever they move to.

Emphasize:
To your players that they need to learn their role positions in the other zone types of defenses.

Run this activity:

At team practice for about 10 minutes for each zone activity, making sure each player gets at least 2 attempts at playing in the different zones. If players are not catching on then you or an assistant coach pull them aside and show them what they are doing wrong so that the practice does not stop and keeps going.

All of these defenses work much in the same way as the *"Man to Man"*, and *"Zone"*, defenses covered in ***SKILL ACTIVITIES 6 THROUGH 25.***

Skill Activity (No.30) The Full Court Press Defense

Object of the activity: Teach all your players how to guard opponents while in a full court defense. Beginning players are not usually allowed to play this type of defense except in only certain situations. But they should still know how to play in it.

What you will need:

You will need a full the court, 2 defenders, 1 inbound player, 1 basketball, 1 coach, and a whistle.

The Basics Are:

This defense is designed to disrupt the opposing teams ability to bring the ball in, and get it up court. In most of the younger age divisions, they have rules that say *"No Press"* allowed in the back court, and 3 feet behind the midcourt line until the opposing team comes into the front court. This is mainly because in the younger divisions, they are more in a training mode. And for a team that is good at it, the full court press can just destroy a young teams confidence in bringing the ball up court from the base line. And they don't get a chance to learn the game when they keep turning the ball over before they ever get a chance to make a shot. Even so you need to be able to show your defender how it works when they do get on a team, later on, that uses it. It is a very good defensive strategy to use when it is legal to use. The reason is, it is an attacking defense that is very disruptive to a team that hasn't practiced breaking the press.

The part we are going to indicate here is bringing the ball in from the back court. How it works is when the opposing team brings the ball in at their end of the court, you usually have two guards, or a guard and one forward, get right in front of the players attempting to bring the ball in. One player stands right in front of the out of bounds player bringing the ball in. They raise their arms, and wave them right in front of the player they are guarding, and jump up and down in an attempt to grab or knock down their inbound pass *(SEE FIGURE 30).* The second player attempts to guard the player, trying to catch the inbound pass, tightly, and if possible they try to make a steal. In some cases both defenders stand right in front of the inbounding player. It will depend on what you want to do.

FIGURE 30

Working the activity:
To practice this play you will need one or two helpers. Then you, or a coach, take the ball and go to a spot out of bounds, at the base line. Or out on the sidewalk in front of the garage. Have your defender get right in front of you, but on the inbound side of the base line. Then they stay right in front of you, waving their arms, trying to knock down or intercept the pass. Have the helper(s) move around behind your defender, and attempt to catch your inbound pass. Remember though you have to

stay in the same spot, and try to make the pass to the helper. You can't go running up and down the base line, trying to get free, so you can make the pass. Practice this play a few times until they get the idea of how it works. But don't spend too much time working on it until your players gets into the upper divisions where the "press" is allowed.

Another way to practice this play is you can also have your defenders tightly guard, and shadow, the loose helper, and attempt to make a steal. However, get another helper to stand in front of you, and wave their arms. On the full court press, the center would usually stay back and closely guard the other center. And the other two players would tightly guard the other two opposing players. The _TIP_ here is while directly trying to knock down or deflect the inbounds pass, make sure your defenders watch only the ball, and not the inbounding players eyes. This way the inbounding player can't head or eye fake them, on where they will throw the inbounds pass.

Emphasize:
To your players that they need to learn how to get their hands way up, wave, and only watch the ball and NOT the inbound player's eyes.

Run this activity:
At team practice for about 15 minutes and making sure each player gets at least 2 attempts at applying the press to the player that inbounds the ball. If players are not catching on then you or an assistant coach pull them aside and show them what they are doing wrong so that the practice does not stop and keeps going.

7. Other Team Defensive Skill Training Activities

Note: ALL ACTIVITIES will be numbered for "EASY " reference.

These drills are more for group orientated training, not just one player at a time. More of your players get to work on these techniques at the same time this way. Let me point out here that you can split up your team into two groups, and work on another drill at the other half of the court at the same time.

Stealing Drills

Skill Activity (No.147) Stealing The Pass Drill
Object of the activity: Teach all your players how to guard opponents and steal passes.
What you will need:
You will need half the court, 1group of defenders, 1 group of receivers, 2 basketballs, 2 coaches, and 2 whistles.
The Basics Are:
The pass receivers have to stay in the same position. The pass stealers have to watch the passers hands and attempt to intercept the ball as it comes out. When P1, P4, get better then spread the receivers out farther and fake the pass some of the time. After about 3 attempts rotate the ball stealers by having them go to the end of the pass receivers line, and pass receivers go to the end of the pass stealers line when they are done. This way everyone gets to work at stealing.
Working the activity:
Have your players line up in 2 groups. The receivers should start out about 10 feet apart to make it easier. You can run this drill out on the two wings where there is room. You have the ball coach. P1 and P4 are the players trying to steal the pass. It's kind of a game of keep away. P2, P3, P5, and P6 are the pass receivers. Give yourself 5 to 10 seconds then blow the whistle and throw the pass to either receiver. The ball stealers attempt to steal the pass.
Emphasize:
To your defenders that they need to learn how to get their hands way up, wave, and only watch the ball and NOT the passing player's eyes.

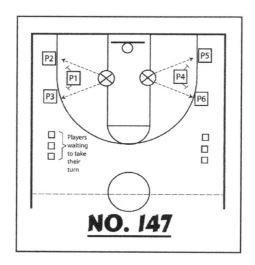

NO. 147

Run this activity:

At team practice for about 15 minutes and making sure each player gets at least 2 attempts at trying to intercept the ball. If players are not catching on then you or an assistant coach pull them aside and show them what they are doing wrong so that the practice does not stop and keeps going.

Skill Activity (No.148) Stealing From the Dribblers Drill

Object of the activity: Teach all your players how to steal the ball from dribbling players.

What you will need:

You will need half the court, 2 groups of defenders, 2 groups of dribblers, 1 basketball, 1 coach, and 1 whistle.

The Basics Are:

This is almost like Drill 145 on Page 13, except the defender can steal the dribbler's ball. It's very hard to learn without fouling, but the little kids have to start somewhere. What this drill will teach them is core memory quickness for reaching in for the ball.

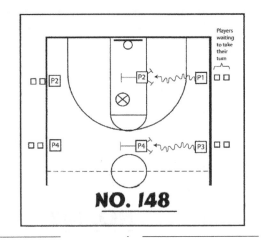

NO. 148

Working the activity:

On your whistle P1 and P3 try to dribble the ball to the other side of the court. P2 and P4 go out and intercept them and attempt to steal the ball. P1 and P3 protect the ball and try to get around P2 and P4. The rule is they can't move more than 5 feet to either side of their central path as they go across. What P2 and P4 have to do is watch the ball as they get close. They have to keep sliding and backing up. They can not touch any part of the dribbler's hands or body if they reach in. As the dribbler moves forward they wait their chance then go for the ball and try to grab it with both hands for a held ball, or knock it away without hitting the dribbler's hands. If P1 or P3 make it to the other side they give the ball to the next player in the line on that side. Then they switch and the dribblers go from that side across court

Emphasize:

To your players that they need to learn how to quickly watch the ball, when the dribbler starts to push the ball down they reach in for the ball. The key is focusing on the ball and NOT the dribbling player or their eyes.

Run this activity:

At team practice for about 15 minutes and making sure each player gets at least 2 attempts at trying to steal the ball away from the dribbler. If players are not catching on then you or an assistant coach pull them aside and show them what they are doing wrong so that the practice does not stop and keeps going.

Rebounding Drills

Skill Activity (No.149) Beginners Rebounding Drill

Object of the activity: Teach all your players how to rebound the ball off the basket..

What you will need:

You will need half the court, 2 groups of rebounders, 1 basketball, 1 coach, and 1 whistle.

The Basics Are:

This is a simple beginners rebounding drill. A player from each group lines up under the basket.

A coach throws the ball up, but misses going in. Both players jump up and try to get the rebound.

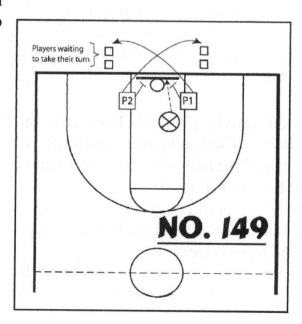

NO. 149

Working the activity:
Have your players line up in 2 groups at the end line. P1 and P2 go under the basket on each side. You stand in front of the basket with the ball. On your whistle you throw up a shot that does not go through the basket. Whichever side the ball rebounds to, that player has to time their jump so that they go up in the air and grab the rebound over their head and before it hits the floor. Players back away from the basket after your shot in case the rebound goes right out in front of the basket. In that case both players have to move over and fight for the rebound. When the rebound is caught or the ball hits the floor the drill is dead. And both players go to the end of the line on the opposite side. By going to the end of the other line the players automatically rotate themselves to the other side of the basket next time. They need to experience how rebounds come off the basket from both sides.

Emphasize:
To your players that they need to learn how to quickly watch the ball and determine where it will come down. The key is focusing on the ball itself and NOT the player throwing it up.

Run this activity:
At team practice for about 15 minutes and making sure each player gets at least 2 attempts at trying to grab the rebound. If players are not catching on then you or an assistant coach pull them aside and show them what they are doing wrong so that the practice does not stop and keeps going.

Skill Activity (No.150) The Circle the Wagons Drill
Object of the activity: Teach all your defenders how to box out and rebound the ball when circling around the basket lane.

What you will need:
You will need half the court, 1 offensive group of 4 players, 1 defensive group of 4 players, 1 basketball, 1 coach, and 1 whistle.

The Basics Are:
Four defenders circle around the lane under the basket. The coach throws the ball up but misses the basket intentionally. Four offensive

70

players out on the 3-point circle rush in, match up with the 4 circling defenders and try to get to the rebound away from the defenders.

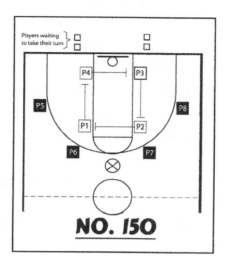

Working the activity:

Have your players line up in 2 groups at the end line, one offensive group and one defensive group. P1, P2, P3, and P4 defenders go under the basket in 2 places on each side of the lane, then they start rotating around the lane (circling). The coach stands in front of the free flow line with the ball. On the whistle the coach throws up a shot that does not go through the basket. Whichever side the ball rebounds to, that player has to time their jump so that they go up in the air and grab the rebound over their head and before it hits the floor. At the same time they need to box out the incoming offensive players trying to get the rebound. Defenders need to back away from the basket after your shot goes up, in case the rebound goes right out in front of the basket. In that case the closest players have to move over and fight for the rebound. When the rebound is caught or the ball hits the floor the drill is dead. And all players go to the end of the other line on the opposite side. By going to the end of the other line the players automatically rotate themselves to the other positions next time and change their roles

Emphasize:

To your players that they need to learn how to quickly watch the ball and determine where it will come down. The key is focusing on the ball itself, and NOT the player or coach throwing it up or their eyes.

Run this activity:

At team practice for about 15 minutes and making sure each player gets at least 2 attempts at trying to grab the rebound as an defensive or offensive player. If players are not catching on then you or an assistant coach pull them aside and show them what they are doing wrong so that the practice does not stop and keeps going.

Skill Activity (No.151) The One On One Rebounding Drill

Object of the activity:

Teach all your players how to box out and rebound the ball one on one.

What you will need:

You will need half the court, 1 offensive group of players, 1 defensive group of players, 1 basketball, 1 coach, and 1 whistle.

The Basics Are:

This is just basically one defensive player going against one offensive player and challenging each other for the ball on the rebound.

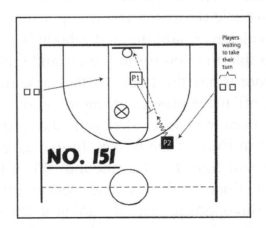

Working the activity:

Have your players line up in 2 groups at each sideline. One group is offense and the other is defense. P2 goes anywhere out on the perimeter, takes 2 or 3 dribbles then takes a perimeter jump shot. P2 can not attempt to drive past P1. When they start to dribble P1 goes out to meet them, and raises their hands in front of them as P2 takes the shot. After the shot P1 boxes out P2 by making butt contact. The defender (P1) makes whatever moves they have to, go right or left, step in the path, hold their position, maintain contact, and look for the ball. Make sure they hustle to pursue the ball. P2 has to try for the rebound also. When one player makes the rebound, both players go to the end of their respective lines. This automatically rotates the players from defense to offense.

Emphasize:

To your players that they need to learn how to quickly watch the ball and determine where it will come down. The key is focusing on the ball itself and NOT the player throwing it up, or their eyes.

Run this activity:

At team practice for about 15 minutes and making sure each player gets at least 2 attempts at trying to grab the rebound as a defensive or offensive player. If players are not catching on then you or an assistant coach pull them aside and show them what they are doing wrong so that the practice does not stop and keeps going.

Skill Activity (No.152) The Dan Maria Rebounding Drill

Object of the activity: Teach all your players how to box out and rebound the ball while in heavy traffic under the basket.

What you will need:

You will need half the court, 3 groups of players, 2 basketballs, 2 coaches, and 2 whistles.

The Basics Are:

This is just basically three defensive players going against each other right under the basket, and challenging each other for rebounding the ball.

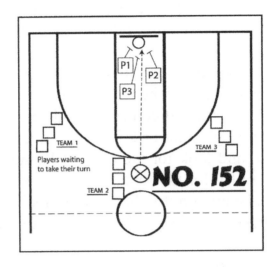

Working the activity:

This is a special former coaches drill for rebounding. You split your team up into 3 groups or teams. Each has to have an equal number of players. Each team lines up outside the 3 point circle and send 1 representative into the 3 second lane (paint). You take a shot at the basket. Whoever gets the rebound returns it to the coach. That player goes to the end of their team's line, and the next player from that line goes into the paint. The players from the other 2 teams stay in the paint until they get a rebound. The first team to have all it's players get a rebound wins. Then the other 2 teams get to run suicides. You could also split your team into two groups and use the basket on the other end of the court. You could also split into two groups and use the other end of the court simultaneously.

Emphasize:

To your players that they need to learn how to quickly watch the ball and determine where it will come down. The key is focusing on the ball itself and NOT the player throwing it up or their eyes.

Run this activity:

At team practice for about 25 minutes and making sure each player gets at least 2 attempts at trying to grab the rebound as a defensive or offensive player. If players are not catching on then you or an assistant coach pull them aside and show them what they are doing wrong so that the practice does not stop and keeps going.

Skill Activity (No.153) The Manhattan College Rebounding Drill

Object of the activity: Teach all your players how to box out and rebound the ball while in heavy traffic under the basket. This is a drill for the bigger kids NOT the beginner little kids because it's too rough.

What you will need:

You will need the full court, 2 groups of players, 2 basketballs, 2 coaches, and 2 whistles.

The Basics Are:

This is just basically three defensive players going against each other right under the basket, and challenging each other for the ball. The other two players can foul whoever gets the rebound while attempting to get to the ball.

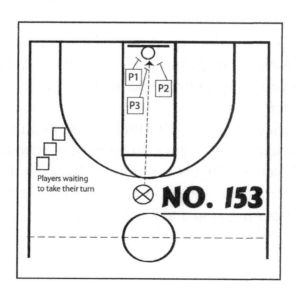

Working the activity:

This is another special former coaches drill for rebounding. This is a drill for the bigger kids, not the little kids. This lets you know who your real scrappy kids are. It's a little too rough for the beginners. You have the ball at the foul line. If you have another coach and enough players you can split into 2 groups at each end of the court. Put 3 players in the paint. You shoot the ball at the basket. All 3 players try for the rebound. Whoever gets the rebound attempts to shoot a basket. The other 2 players are allowed to foul the rebounder to keep them from scoring. However it can't be a flagrant foul, but they should be physical.

When one of the players makes their basket, the ball becomes live again as soon as it goes through the net. The first player that scores 3 times gets to go out, then a new player joins the other remaining 2. The remaining 2 players start back at zero baskets (scores). This drill teaches toughness. This goes continuous because the ball is always live, so 10 minutes of this under the basket and the remaining players that can't score are "gassed." You could also split the team and work simultaneously on the other end of the court

Emphasize:

To your players that they need to learn how to quickly watch the ball and determine where it will come down. The key is focusing on the ball itself and NOT the player throwing it up or their eyes. This is a rough survival type drill so your players better be in shape physically.

Run this activity:

At team practice for about 30 minutes and making sure each player gets at least 2 attempts at trying to grab the rebound as a defensive or offensive player. If players are not catching on then you or an assistant coach pull them aside and show them what they are doing wrong so that the practice does not stop and keeps going.

Shot Blocking Drills

Skill Activity (No.154) The One on One Shot Blocking Drill
Object of the activity: Teach all your players how to block shots when they are one on one with the opponent.
What you will need:
You will need the full court, 4 groups of players, 2 basketballs, 2 coaches, and 2 whistles.
The Basics are:
This is just basically 1 shot block defender and 2 other defenders waiting to catch a blocked ball from a dribbler taking a shot at the basket.
Working the activity:
Have your players line up in 2 groups, one on each sideline. One group is offense and the other is defense. P2 goes anywhere out on the perimeter, takes only 4 dribbles then has to make a perimeter jump shot. P2 can not attempt to drive past P1. When they start to dribble P1 goes out to meet them. They have to watch very carefully to time their block. They can block the shot just as P2 starts to bring it up to shoot and it's still in their hand, or they can try to block it in the air as it comes off P2's hand. What they have to learn to do is block it and push it to either P3 or P4 as opposed to swatting it out of bounds. After 2 blocks rotate all players, and make sure your taller centers and forwards always get their blocking attempts in. You could also split the team and work simultaneously on the other end of the court.

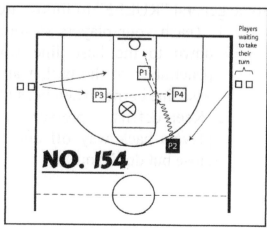

NO. 154

Emphasize:

To your players that they need to learn how to quickly watch the ball and determine where it will come off the shooters hand then time their jump.

Run this activity:

At team practice for about 15 minutes and making sure each player gets at least 2 attempts at trying to block the shot and swat it to a teammate. If players are not catching on then you or an assistant coach pull them aside and show them what they are doing wrong so that the practice does not stop and keeps going.

8. Defensive Plays

Note: ALL ACTIVITIES will be numbered for "EASY " reference.
There are half court defensive plays, full court defensive plays, out of bounds defensive plays, fast break defensive plays, delay defensive plays, and tip off defensive plays. We will show some good "man to man" pressure defenses, and zone defenses.

Half Court Defensive Plays

Man to Man Defenses

Man to Man Pressure

Some general "RULES" to follow are:

1. Teach your players to force the ball to the sideline, and then down to the base line when at all possible. Do not allow penetration to the basket along the base line. Try to trap at the base line corner when possible.
2. Keep defensive pressure on the ball at all times. Don't let your players back way off and let the opponent move around. Get close but don't foul.

3. Have your players let the opponents point guard pass out to the wings, but don't let them pass back to the point guard in the middle.

4. Have your players deny dribble penetration along the base line. Tell them to take a charging foul if necessary. If the defender on the dribbler gets beaten, your lo-post defender, who is fronting the opponent's lo-post, has to immediately rotate to the base line to stop the dribbler.

5. Make it difficult for the opponents outside shooters to get a shot off. Have your players get their hands up high in front of the shooter.

6. Tell your players not to reach in unless they are really good at it, if not they will probably get the foul called on them. And as they reach in they are off balance, and that might let the opponent hook them and go around. If they do reach in, tell them to reach in on the inside (middle of the court side) of the opponent, forcing them to go more to the outside of the court, away from the basket.

7. Teach your players to use "help and recover" techniques. This means your teammates come over to "help" your player if they do get beaten by the opponent. This givesthem time to "recover" and get back to their man.

Defensive Positioning off the Ball
Position No.1 (No.72)

Many teams come down and go into a 2 in, 3 out offense. First tell your players to pretend there is an imaginary line up the middle of the court, called the "help side line" (shown as the heavy line splitting the paint). Then also have them imagine an imaginary line drawn from the ball to each offensive player (shown as a dotted line). Then each player locates, called one pass away, in a "deny" mode, and stays on the dotted line. Your No.4 and No.5 players take the lo-post opponents. Your No.2 stays right on the opponents No.2. Your No.1 stays right on the opponents No.1. Your No.3 player locates at the weak side free throw line elbow.

No.3 will let the pass go to their No.3 out on the wing, but as soon as their No.3 gets the pass they go out and get right on them so that they can not pass the ball back over to their No.1 at the top of the key. If you decide you want to deny the pass to their No.3 out on the wing, you have your No.3 move over on the dotted line and front them.

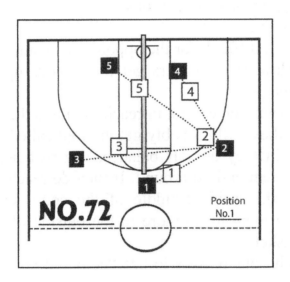

Position No.2 (No.73)

The defenders (your No.3 and No.5 players), located as two passes away, are called "help side" players. When the ball gets down in the corner, they are located with one foot on the "help side" line. It helps them prevent inside passing, and dribble penetration. Tell them to use their peripheral vision, to always keep sight of the ball and their man. Some coaches call this the "pistol" positions. You can illustrate this to them by having them use both of their index fingers pointed as if shooting a gun. First one finger at the ball, then the other finger pointed at the man, with both arms out stretched. Another term coaches will use for this is, the "ball-you-man" positioning. Your No.1, 2, and 4, players slide over and front their man opponents, staying on the dotted line.

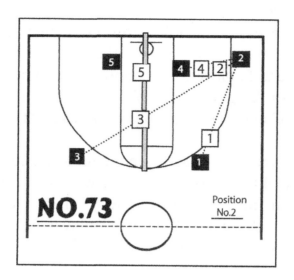

NO.73

Position
No.2

Position No.3 (No.74)

Your No.5 is now in a good position to deny the backside lob over pass to their No.5 at the lo- post, or dribble penetration by their No.2. No.4 blocks No.2. Take notice (from play No.72 and 73) of how your No.5 and No.3 rotate when the ball moves to the corner. Also take notice that whenever the ball is below the free throw line, the "help side" defenders (your No.3 and No.5) have one foot on the help side line.

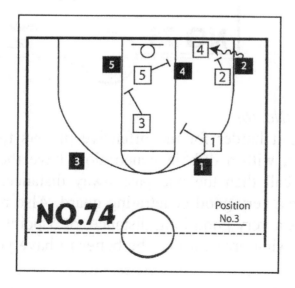

NO.74

Position
No.3

Position No.4 (No.75)

When a bounce pass or a lob throw goes over to the offensive No.3 player out on the wing, notice how the defense shifts and rotates over. Your No.1, 3, and 5, players stay on the dotted line. Your No.4 and No.1 are on the center "help side line". Your No.2 is kind of splitting the distance between their No.2 offensive man, and along the edge of the lane.

If offensive player No.4 makes a move up to the left side free throw line elbow, your No.4 moves right up along with them. What they try to do is get one hand in front of them to "deny" them the pass from offensive player No. 3 on the wing. Your No.2 player has to be ready to move towards offensive player No.4 in case a lob pass goes over to them from offensive player No.3.

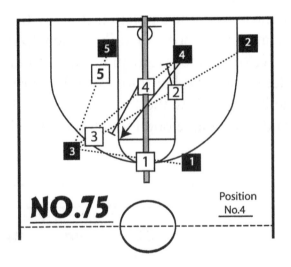

NO.75

Position No.4

Position No.5 (No.76)

To help make it harder for the offensive players to beat your players guarding them, with a dribble penetration, have them get a few steps closer to the ball than the one pass away distance. Do this when the opposition has a very good penetrating guard. Also remember that if the opposition has a very good long distance, or 3 point shooter located out on one of the wing areas, it may be better to have your player guarding them go back in a "deny" position, and not leave them to give help. Normally when the offensive No.3 player tries to dribble penetrate, your No.1 player has to come over and give help.

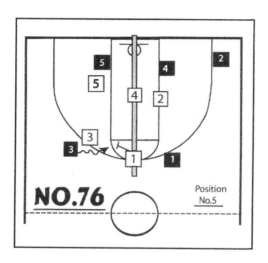

NO.76

Position No.5

Position No.6 (No.77)

This play as well as No.76 show how to give help and recover on the perimeter areas. When offensive player No.3 is denied dribble penetration, they have to pass the ball out to their No.1 player. Your defender player No.1 has to move out quickly to the on ball "deny" position. Your No.3 player stays in the "deny" position while your No.2 and No.4 players move quickly to their "deny" positions. Your No.5 player moves to their "help side" position. In teaching "help and recover," tell your players to move their feet quickly to establish position, and prevent the dribble move. What they *don't* want to do is reach in and get a foul called on them..

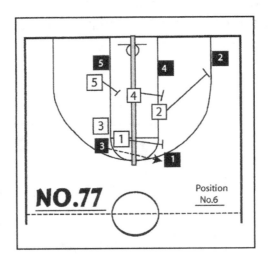

NO.77   Position No.6

Defending Post Players

Position No.7 (No.78)

Coaches say make every effort to keep the ball out of the low post. Two things usually happen (both bad) when the offense gets the ball into the lo-post, the first is they score, and second is a defender commits a foul. Most coaches say 1/2 to 3/4 front the offensive lo-post player (No.4) from the base line side, if they are taller. That is keeping one foot between the player and the basket, and one hand as a bar in front of them.

If they are shorter though, a full front position is advised. Teach your lo-post defensive players to work on their good footwork. They will have to be quick and agile to "deny" offensive lo-post players.

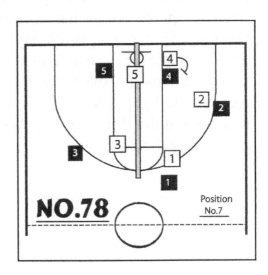

NO.78   Position No.7

Position No.8 (No. 79)

When the offensive player No.2 can't get the ball into their No.4, they will pass back to their No.1. As soon as your No.4 player can see the ball go over to offensive player No.1 out at the point, they move around to the inside and 1/2 to 3/4 front offensive player No.4. They also keep both feet to the side, and use one arm in front to bar the pass.

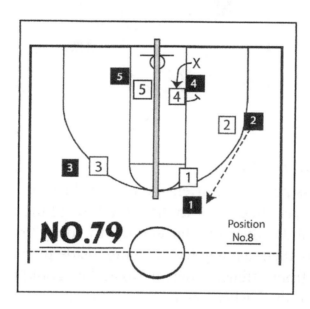

NO.79

Position
No.8

Position No.9 (No.80)

What your player No.4 wants to do is hold their 1/2 to 3/4 front position on offensive player No.4 (shown in dotted). What they *don't* want to do is go all the way around front on the top (shown in solid) because this will let No.4 get the ball and hook them on the inside, to go to the basket.

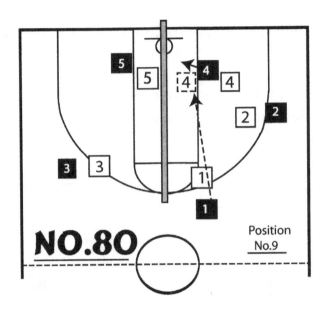

NO.80

Position No.9

Position No.10 (No.81)

When the pass goes from offensive player No.1 out to No.2 on the wing, your No.3 player slides over to the left elbow of the free throw line. Your No.4 player slides over just far enough to "deny" offensive No.4 player to pin or hook them as they try take the inside path to the basket. If your No.4 tries to front offensive player No.4, they could get the pass and have an easy spin to the basket (see position No.9).

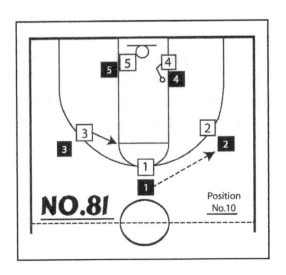

NO.81

Position No.10

Position No.11 (No.82)

When a pass does go in to offensive No.4, your No.4 holds their position No.10) and still "denies" No.4 the base line. Your No.3 player quickly comes down to help, "denying" offensive No.4 the inside move to the basket. Offensive No.4 will then probably have to kick the ball back out to their No.1 or No.2. This should keep the opponents lo-post from making an easy basket.

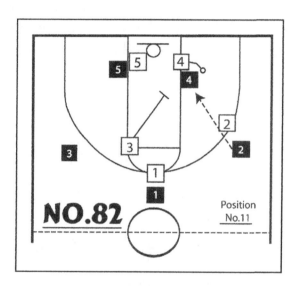

Defending Cutters

Most defensive minded coaches say, you should always "deny" a pass to a cutter moving through the lane. Basically all defenders need to stay between their man and the ball._One technique some defenders use is to "bump the cutter" off of their intended pathway. They do this by getting position on the cutter, then riding them away from the basket. This is a special skill you will have to work on, by practicing with them. Teach them to beat the cutter to a certain spot on the floor, by observing as they move, to where they think the cutter is going. Both players are entitled to that certain spot on the floor it just depends on who gets there first. Teach them this kind of thinking. Many times you can get "charging" called.

General cuts to defend are, cuts from the weak side wing (with or without screens), "give and go's", flash cuts to either hi or lo-post, and back-cuts. Teach your players to recognize them.

Position No.12 (No.83)
A special cut sometimes used is the "curl-cut". Defending against this offensive play (not to common) is going to take a fast, and smart player. First they will have to recognize it, then second follow it. The offensive player No.2 makes a cut to the basket. Your No.2 has to "chase" them all the way around offensive No.4, and back out to the 3 point circle.

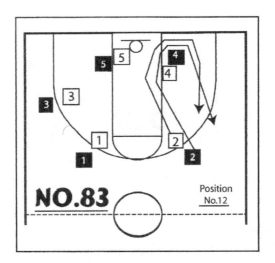

Position No.13 (No.84)
What can happen is if your No.2 gives up the "chase" and waits to pick them up when they come back around, offensive No.2 goes to the corner and is clear for a 3 point shot. Then offensive player No.1 lobs a long pass over to them for the shot.

Defending Against Screens

Most defensive minded coaches say, you must have a plan against "screens". If you don't, a good team will see that and make your players really look bad. As you can probably see by now is, screens are a big part of the offensive play book. Inside screens should be switched between your No.4 and No.5 players because you probably won't have a size, or quickness, mismatch. On outside perimeter screens, you will have to decide, depending on the team you are playing, whether you want to "switch," "fight through them," or "slide" under them. Switching on perimeter screens can lead to a size or quickness mismatch match. This is especially true when a big post player steps outside to set a screen for a guard.

On-Ball Screens

Position No.14 (No.85)

The opponents No.2 player has the ball. It's a case when you can probably fight over the screen rather than "switching." Your No.1 comes over and fakes a switch by stepping out against offensive player No.3. What this does is "deny" No.3 to go up the lane, and forces them to go outside. That lets your No.3 to fight over the top of the screen, and stay on the opponent. Your No.1 must quickly go back to covering their man. Again this is another example of "help and recover." These are also plays that you have to teach your players to communicate with each other on.

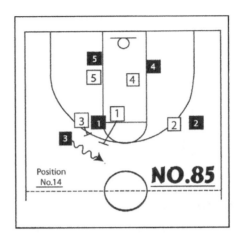

Off-Ball Screen

Position No.15 (No.86)
Offensive player No.2 has the ball. In this play your No.3 has dropped down to the left side of the free throw line at "help side," Offensive player No.3 starts to move over and break for a drive down the lane. Offensive player No.1 comes right at your No.3 for a screen or block. What your No.1 player has to do is move over to help. This forces offensive player No.3 go out wider at the top of the key. And this leaves more room for your No.3 to fight over the top of the screen, and stay with offensive player No.3 as they move across. Your No.1 has to then slide back over and stay with their No.1.

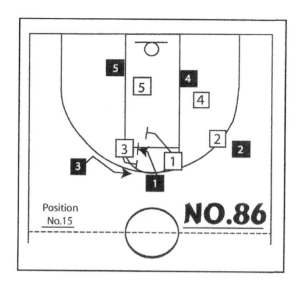

Position No. 16 (No.87)

One of the other alternatives is, your No.3 player rolls off the screen and slides under and around the screener, to stay with offensive player No.3. Then your No.1 stays with their No.1.

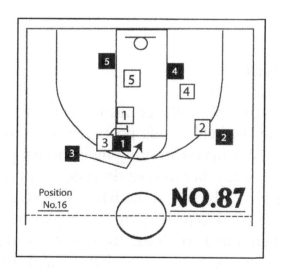

Position No. 17 (No.88)

The other alternative is to "switch," where your No.1 stays with their No.3, and your No.3 stays with their No.1. The problem is during the "switch," your No.3 has to step under and be careful not to get sealed off on the outside, letting their No.1 to roll off on the inside and down towards the basket.

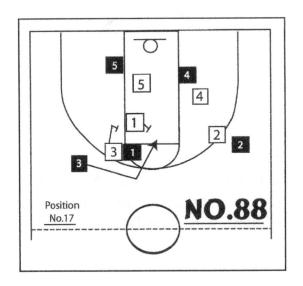

Inside Post Screen

Position No. 18 (No.89)

When the opponents No.2 player has the ball on the wing, most coaches say it is better to "switch" inside post screens. Here is the rule your post players follow. Your player fronting their lo-post player always takes the low cutter while your other lo-post defender always takes the high cutter. The opponents No.2 player has the ball. Offensive player No.5 cuts low. Offensive player No.4 screens your No.5 player away from the cutter. Your No.4 switches and continues to front offensive player No.5 as they come around. Your No.5 player "switches" and follows No.4, after they screen, as they break towards the right side of the lane.

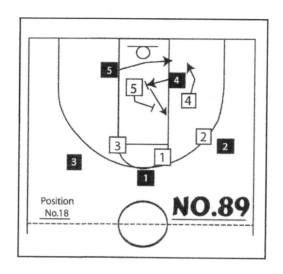

Position
No.18

NO.89

Position No. 19 (No.90)

Offensive player No.5 cuts high (most common move) to the right side of the lane. Your No.4 "switches" and moves down the lane to cover No.5, and deny them the pass from No.2. Offensive player No.4 screens your player No.5, who drops low to cover offensive player No.4 on the "switch,"

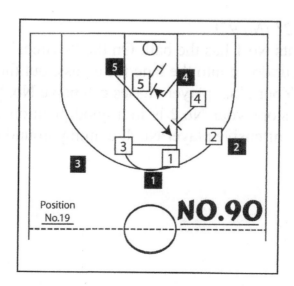

Position
No.19

NO.90

Position No.20 (No.91)

Sometimes the "switch" is not necessary. When offensive player No.5 cuts high, your No.5 moves up the lane and over the top of the screen to cover them from the pass from offensive player No.2. Your player No.4 just slides over, and continues to front offensive player No.4 as they attempt to screen No.5.

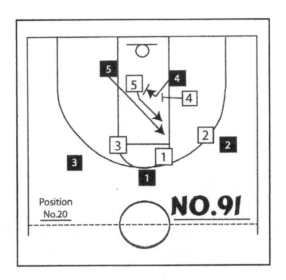

Down screens

Position No.21 (No.92)

The opponents No.1 has the ball. On the "switch," offensive player No.2 pretends to cut down into the lane for a pass, but then screens and blocks your No.4 . Your No.2 player chases offensive No.2 into the lane. When the screener stops your No.2 is in a good position to "switch," and pick up the cutter, offensive player No.4, coming around the screen.

94

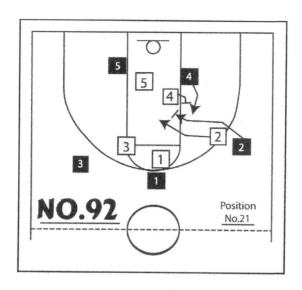

NO.92

Position No.21

Position No.22 (No.93)

There can be a problem though. This is what could happen if the "switch" is made. The first problem is there could be a big-little mismatch match when your No.2 starts to cover offensive player No.4. The second problem can happen if offensive player No.4 reads the "switch," turns, and cuts out to the right wing for a pass from offensive player No.1. In that case your No. 2 player could easily get trapped and caught inside. This leaves offensive player No.4 open, out on the perimeter, for a jumper or a 3 point shot.

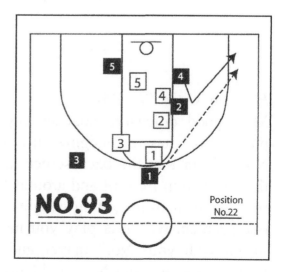

NO.93

Position No.22

Back screens

Position No.23 (No. 94)

The opponents No.1 has the ball. This is a so called "back-door" cut to the basket. The offensive player No.2 cuts around offensive player No.4 and heads for the basket. Offensive player No. 4 moves out towards the perimeter and screens your player No.2. Your player No.4 will "switch," and cover offensive player No.2 from getting a pass on the inside.

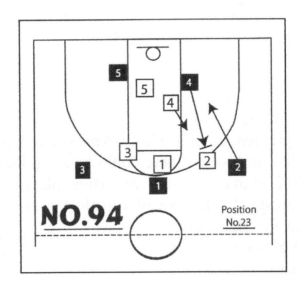

Position No.24 (No. 95)

Most good defensive coaches say make this "switch" instead. Your player No.4 has to recognize the back-door play, and call out to your No.2 player that the back screen is coming. What your No.2 has to do then is, step in front of and around No.4 to get inside positioning. This is to keep them from getting caught on the outside of the screen. There is one problem with this play you may end up with a big-little mismatch match with your No.2 player and offensive player No.4. So the first chance they get, your No.2 and No.4 want to "switch" back to the players they were guarding. If the ball goes over to the weak side, then that is a good time to make the "switch" back. Meanwhile your No.4 player, recognizing the back screen, steps over, picks up offensive player cutting to the basket and stays right with them. This prevents offensive No.1 from making a pass or lob throw to them for the lay up, or jumper.

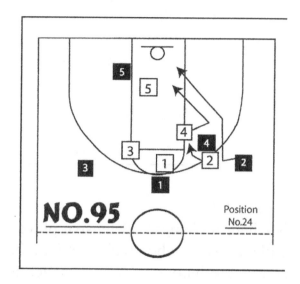

NO.95

Position No.24

Out of Bounds Defenses

Many coaches like to play the base line out of bounds, with a 2-3 zone. Here is a good man-to-man pressure defense to especially keep from getting burned inside.

Man-to-Man Box

Position No.1 (No.96)

This is called the "box out of bounds" play. If you look at it, is really just the "box and 1" turned around at the base line. The exception is your No.3 plays a one man zone to "deny" passes inside around the basket. The rest of your players form a box and guard the lane for any inside short passes to the offensive inside players.

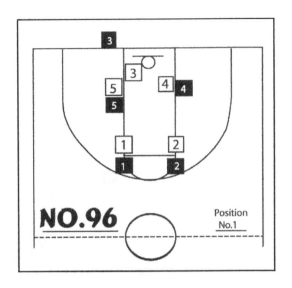

NO.96

Position No.1

Position No.2 (No.97)

Now here is where it changes. Offensive player No.3 passes the ball out to offensive player No.1, who breaks out into the left wing area to get the pass. As soon as the inbounds pass is made, and offensive player No.3 breaks for the left corner, your No.3 player breaks and moves out to cover No.3, using a man-to-man defense to cover them. As soon as offensive player No.1 gets the ball they will pass it out to No.3 in the corner. Offensive player No.5 attempts to screen your player No.4. Offensive player No.4 breaks into the lane for a possible inside pass.

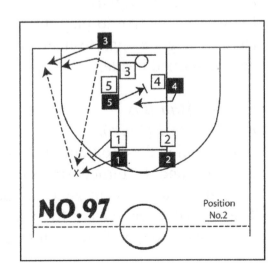

NO.97

Position No.2

Position No.3 (No.98)

Your No.4 and No.5 post players "switch" on the screen. Your player No.4 "switches", and steps around and under No.5's screen, to get inside positioning. Your No.5 "switches", and picks up offensive No.4 breaking into the lane. Offensive No.1 and No.2 will probably stay out on the perimeter through all this, as a safety to get the inbounds pass. Just let them get the ball if they are open way out on the perimeter. They are usually the shooters with little kids teams, and it's harder for them to make the long outside shots. Then reload and go into your regular defense, zone or whatever.

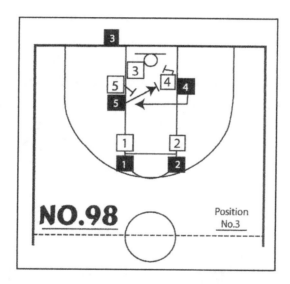

Man-to-Man Stack

This is a tough offensive "out of bounds" play to defense, especially for the little kids. There are so many different ways to offensively load this positioning. Players can go different ways, and they can be put in different locations within the stack. We will not try to show every possibility, but we will show a number of ways the opponents will try to trick you and get open. If you can break right with them, protect the basket inside, and keep them from making the inbounds pass for too long of time (5 seconds), they may make a mistake and make a bad pass you can intercept for a steal. The idea with the man-to-man defense is stay right with them as close as you can without fouling them.

Position No.1 (No.99)

I like the 3 in 2 out basic defense against the "stack". Usually the offense has 2 or 3 plays off the stack. The offensive out of bounds ball holder will hold up 1, 2, or 3, fingers as to which play they want to run. They will yell, "BREAK," and the players all move. What you want your players to do is break with them if possible. In this particular play, offensive player No.2 breaks for the left wing corner, to get a quick inbounds pass from No.1. After throwing in the ball, their No.1 breaks for the right wing corner, to open up the left lo-post area. Your No.1 follows. Their No.5 breaks the opposite way to the right lo-post. Your No.5 has to slide over with them, but stay on the "help line." Your No.2 moves out to stay on their No.2. Their No.4 then tries to cut down to the left lo-post. Your No.4 has to move down with them so that they will not get open at the left lo-post. Their No.3 cuts to the left wing perimeter, to be open for a safety valve inbounds pass. Your No.3 has to stay right with them.

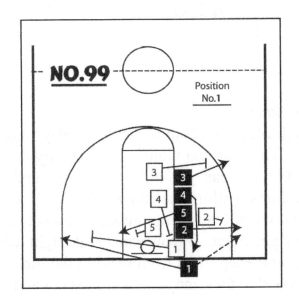

Position No.2 (No.100)

Sometimes the defense will send their No.3 out of bounds to make the pass. This is to free up guards No.1 and No.2 to get the inbounds pass. Both of them break to the left wing 3 point circle. Your No.1 and No.2 players have to break with them, and stay close. Their No.4 player will break to the right side of the lane, hoping to pull your No.4 with them, to free up some space. Your No.4 has to slide across, but stay on the "help line". Their No.5 player cuts straight down to the left lo-post. Your No.5 drops down to cover, but also stays on the "help line." Their No.3 inbounds the ball to their No.1 as soon as they break, and get clear. Your No.1 closes on them, then and stays right with them, denying them the inside route to the basket. After their No.3 makes the inbounds pass, they cut to the right side corner. Your No.3 has to move out with them, so they are not wide open for a long 3 point shot.

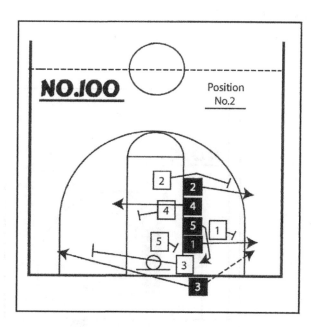

Position No.3 (No.101)

Sometimes teams will stack up on the right side edge of the lane, instead of the left side. This is to confuse your defense. It's still the same sideways break of some kind though. And if you notice, it's still basically your center and the 2 forwards (3 in) around the lane, and your 2 guards (2 out) are on the perimeter. It's just where they locate each time is going to depend on where their counterpart offensive players are within the stack. You have to teach your players to recognize what is happening, and then cover their counterpart players. Also teach them to communicate to each other what is happening. Their No.3 inbounds to their No.1 then cuts to the left wing corner. Your No.3 follows. Your No.1 moves right out to cover their No.1. Their No.2 breaks for the top of the right wing area. Your No.2 follows. Their No.4 and No.5 players both break towards the left wing side, hoping to pull your No. 4 and No.5 with them. This is to free up open space around the basket, for their No.1 to try and drive the lane and score. Your players move out to the edge, but keep one foot on the "help line".

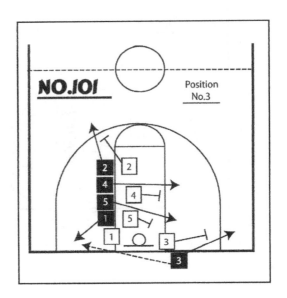

Position No.4 (No.102)

Here again, their No.3 takes the ball out of bounds, to try and get the ball to their quicker guards (No.1 and No.2). Notice how they move their No.1 up in the stack so that they can get free out on the wing. This is what you have to recognize from the bench, and your players out on the court. The offense will usually only have a few plays, you have to figure out from the bench where they are putting their players in the stack, then communicate that to your players on the court. Their No.3 inbounds to their No.1 out on the wing then cuts to the left wing corner. Your No.3 follows.

Your No.1 has to be ready to move right out to cover their No.1 as soon as they notice No.1 higher up in the stack. The "CLUE" is that's why they are higher up in the stack, so they can get clear on the wing for the inbounds pass. Their No.4 and No.5 players both break towards the left wing side, hoping to pull your No. 4 and No.5 with them out on the wing. Again, this is to free up open space around the basket, for their No.1 to drive the lane, or try a short jump shot. Their No.2 breaks for the top left wing area as a safety valve, in case No.1 is covered, for the inbounds pass. Your No.2 follows.

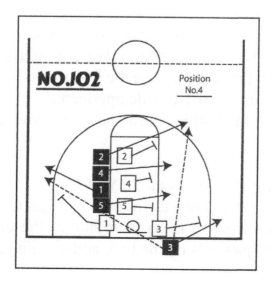

Zone Defenses

The 1-3-1 Zone Trap

This is a very common half court defense. To understand how this works, you will have to explain to your players about how the court is divided up into the zones. The half court is divided up, above and below the free throw line, and down the middle with a left side and a right side.

Here are your player "RULES:"

For your Point (1), Middle (4), Bottom (5) players (No.103)

For all 3 players, the court is divided into above the free throw line, and below the free throw line. Special "RULES" for your No.1 (point) player are:

1. When the ball is above the free throw line they play right on the ball.
2. When the ball is below the free throw line, your No.1 swings around and "denies" any passes out of the corner.

Special "RULES" for your No.4 (middle) player are:

1. When the ball is above the free throw line, they "deny" any pass into the hi-post area.
2. When the ball is below the free throw line, No.4 "denies" any passes into the ball side lo-post area.

Special "RULES" for your No.5 (bottom) player are:

1. When the ball is above the free throw line, your No.5 is blocking in front of the ball side opponent.
2. When the ball is below the free throw line, your No.5 is on the ball.

For your Wing Players 2 and 3 (No.103)

The court is divided down the middle with a left side and a right side:

1. When the ball is on their side of the court, your No.2 or No.3 (wing) player is on the ball, and guarding.

2. When the ball is above the free throw line and on the other side of the court, your No.2 or No.3 player "denies" the cross court pass.

3. When the ball is below the free throw line and on the other side of the court, your No.2 or No.3 player "denies" the pass into the ball side hi-post area.

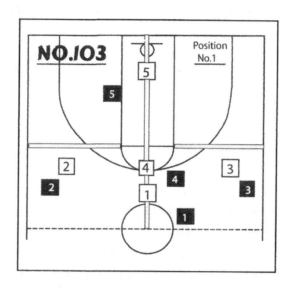

When the Ball is in the Top Corners (No.104)
When the ball is in the top right corner, your No.1 and No.3 move over to trap offensive player No.1. The players legs should be crossed and interlocked so that No.1 can't dribble the ball out. Your No.2 player moves over towards the top of the key, and "denies" any cross court passes. Your No.4 "denies" any passes into the right hi-post. Your No.5 "denies" any passes into the right lo-post. When the ball is in the top left corner your No.1 and No.2 move over to trap offensive player No.1. Your No.3 player moves over towards the top of the key, and "denies" any cross court passes. Your No.4 "denies" any passes into the left hi-post. Your No.5 "denies" any passes into the left lo-post.

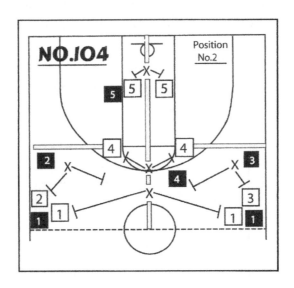

When the Ball is in the Bottom Corners (No.105)

When the ball is in the bottom right corner, your No.3 and No.5 move over to trap offensive player No.1. The players legs should be crossed and interlocked so that No.1 can't dribble the ball out. Your No.1 player moves over towards the right wing, and "denies" any passes back out from No.1 into the right wing area. Your No.2 "denies" any passes into the right hi-post. Your No.4 moves down and "denies" any passes into the right lo-post. When the ball is in the bottom left corner, your No.2 and No.5 move over to trap offensive player No.1. Your No.1 player moves over towards the left wing area, and "denies" any passes back out from No.1 into the left wing area. Your No.3 "denies" any passes into the left hi-post. Your No.4 moves down and "denies" any passes into the left lo-post.

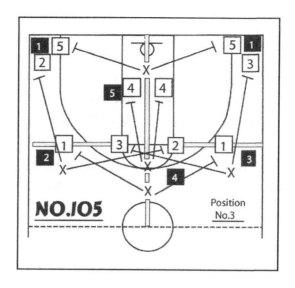

NO.105

Position No.3

When the Ball gets into the High Post (No.106)

This is how your players react if the ball does get into the hi-post. Your wing player No.3 sprints down to the weak side lo-post as soon as they see the pass start to go into offensive player No.2 at the hi-post. Your players No.1 and No.2 quickly move to the weak side hi-post area, and the strong side free throw elbow. Your No.4 player reacts, and stops offensive player No.2 from dribbling into the lane. If you notice, this has sort of formed into a 3-2 zone defense.

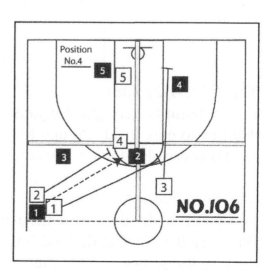

Position No.4

NO.106

When the Ball gets into the Lo-Post (No.107)
Tell your players to do everything they can to keep the ball from getting into the lo-post. But if it does, this is how your players react. Offensive player No.1 is trapped and has the ball in the corner. They manage to get a pass into offensive player No.2. As soon as your player No.2 player can see the pass go in to offensive player No.2, they sprint to the weak side lo-post. Your No.4 player has to "deny" offensive player No.2 the dribble or a shot until help gets there. Your players No.3 and No.5 sprint to the low lane area for "help." Your No.1 quickly moves to the right free throw elbow, to fill the spot that was occupied by No.2.

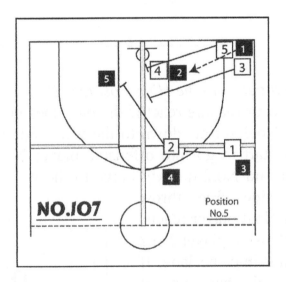

NO.107

Position
No.5

The 2-3 (2-1-2) Zone
This defense is very good against a team with big kids, or slower kids, that like to play inside around the basket. However, it can be beaten by a team that can shoot good from the outside.

The Positioning (No.108)
The court is divided up a little differently than the 1-3-1 zone setup. Basically the court is divided into below the free throw line, and above the free throw line. Above the free throw line the court is divided down

the middle, with a left half and a right half. Below the free throw line the court is divided into 3 areas (zones), the middle, the left side, and the right side.

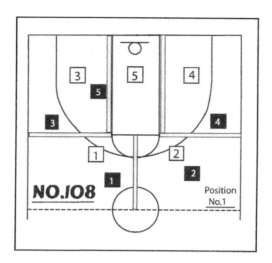

When Ball is on the Wings (No.109)

When the ball goes to the right wing, the zone flip-flops and rotates, with the guards sliding over to the right. Your No.2 player has to stay right on their player No.2, to make it hard for them to dribble or pass the ball off. Notice that your No.1 player has moved over to the strong side free throw elbow.

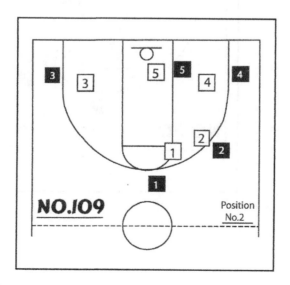

Trapping the Corners (No.110)

When the ball goes to the right corner, the zone flip-flops and rotates, with a guard and a forward moving over to trap offensive player No.4 in the corner. On the right corner (shown), your players No.2 and No.4 have moved over to trap offensive player No.4. Your No.1 has slid over, taking the place of your No.2, to guard offensive player No.2 on the wing. They also have to "deny" a pass to either offensive player No.2, or No.1, trying to cut down the right side of the lane. Your No.3 has moved over to the top of the lane, below the free throw line.

They have to guard against, and "deny", any passes to either offensive player No.1, or offensive player No.3 across court at the weak side lo-post. Your No.5 has to quickly move into a lo-post blocking position to "deny" a pass in to offensive player No.5 at the strong side lo-post. If they do not get there in time, it may be an easy pass, then lay-up, or short jump shot, for offensive player No.5 to make.

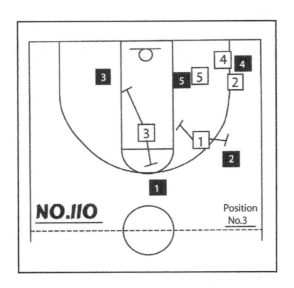

NO.110 Position No.3

110

Passes from Corners out to Wings (No.111)

When the ball is in the right corner, the zone flip-flops and rotates, with a guards and a forwards moving over to the right side. On the right corner (shown), your player No.4 guards and blocks against a dribble to the basket. Your No.2 player guards and blocks offensive player No.2 from getting a pass back out into the wing area. Your No.1 player moves to the right elbow of the free throw line, to block any moves down and into the lane. Your No.3 moves back over to the middle of the lane. They have to be ready to either move quickly to the basket, or out to the perimeter, to cover or "deny" long passes. Your No.5 closely guards offensive player No.5 from getting the ball, then turning and dribbling the ball to the basket.

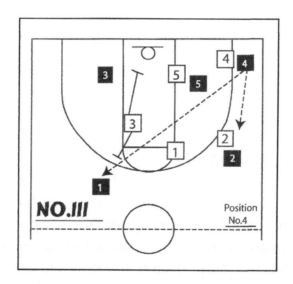

NO.III

Position No.4

Passes into the Hi-Post (No.112)

When the pass comes into the hi-post, your No.5 player has to come up and defend the top of the key. Notice that when your No.5 comes up, this starts to look like a 2-1-2 defense. What your No.3 has to watch for is, offensive player No.2 cutting and sneaking in under the basket for a shot.

In fact both your No.3 and No.4 players may have to cheat into the lane, to cover after your No.5 moves up towards the hi-post. Your No.1 covers their No.3 and No.4.

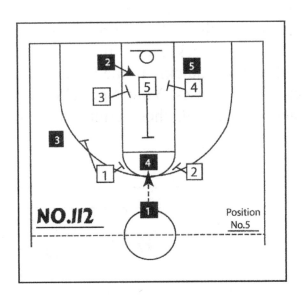

Defending the Point (No.113)

This is always a tough area to guard while in a zone defense. If you know the opponents No.2 is their best shooter then have your No.1 defend the point area at first. Then have your No.2 sag over towards their No.2 (shown). However if their No.1 starts hitting some shots from the point, then your No.1 is going to have to come out and pressure them. This is just flip-flopped if their No.3 is their best shooter. Tell your No.1 and No.2 players to never let the opponents No.1 split between them, and dribble down the middle.

You are going to have to teach both your No.1 and No.2 to work hard, and move quickly to cover both the wings and the point. Your No.3, 4, and 5, players will have to rotate as shown as the ball moves to the opposite side of the court. On ball reversal, your No.3 player "helps" by coming out a short distance when the ball gets out to the wing on their side, then quickly drops back down to cover the lo-post. Your No.5 has to be ready to slide down to the middle of the lane to "help".

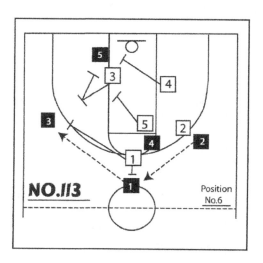

Covering Corner Skip Passes (No.114)
When the ball is in the right corner, your No.1 has to cover both the opponents No.1 or No.3 as soon as they know which player is getting the skip pass on the point or wing. If the ball is in the left corner, your No.2 has to do the covering at the point and right wing.

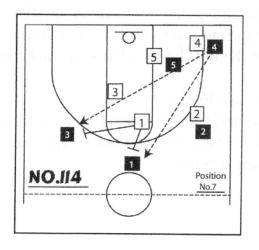

113

Covering Double Teamed Corner Skip Passes (No. 115)
When the ball is in the right corner, your No.3 has to cover both the corner or the wing as soon as they know which one is getting the pass. When the pass goes to the opponents No.1 at the point, your No.1 has to move out and pressure them.

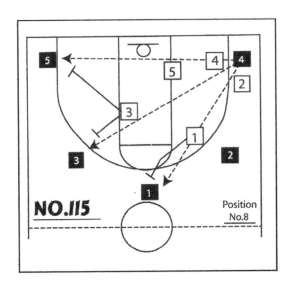

Delay Defenses

The 4 Corner Stopper
Coach what you are going to have to do first is figure out why the opponent is going into a delay. If it's late in the game call a time out if possible, and let the kids know what you want them to do, so it's clear to them.
Here are some possible reasons:

       1. It's a young team, a low scoring game, the opponent is ahead in the score. There is 2 minutes or so on the clock. They are afraid your team is better.

2. The opponent can't penetrate your zone defense, they want to try and force you out on the perimeter to open up inside space so they can score.

3. Both teams are good scoring teams, there is a minute or less on the clock, they are ahead by only a few points.

4. They are going for the last shot in the quarter, or the game.

After you figure out why, then you can use several strategies:

If you decide they are doing this because of reason No.1, then the best thing to do is go right out quickly and put light pressure on them, don't let them dribble around, try to make a steal, double team trap, and don't foul. Get the ball back as quick as you can.
Make them take the long shots. Young kids are not so good at this.

If you decide this is because of reason No.2, then take your time, and go out and put soft pressure on them. If you are ahead, they are the team that's in the hurry. Don't help them out by rushing. Tell your players don't let them dribble around them, or cut to the basket because that's what they are going to try and do.

If you decide this is because of reason No.3, then go out and quickly put pressure on them, and try not to foul. You have to have to get the ball back so you can score. Sometimes when they see the ball go out to one of the corners, your 2 closest outside players can move in quickly and run a trap. Also with young teams the trap can sometimes cause them to get exited and make a turnover pass.

If you decide this is because of reason No.4, then go out quickly and put pressure on them, and try not to foul. If you are ahead, take your time and play soft, but don't let them score. A trap might run down the clock if you have the players quick enough to get there and run it. If you are behind, and desperately need to score quickly, then you are going to have to make a steal, or trap, just to get the ball back.

Motion No.1 (No.116)
So what you want to do is start in a 2-1-2 defensive set, then go from there. At the youth level, what the offense is probably going to use this

for is stalling, that's what the 4 corners does. It usually starts with an offensive guard (No.1) dribbling in to the point. Then they just stay there until you send a player out to pressure them (No.1). The other thing their No.1 will do is, pass the ball around out to their perimeter players (No.2, 3, 4, and 5). Tell your No.2, 3, 4, and 5, perimeter players to keep looking *quickly* back and forth, between the ball handler and the player they are guarding. They might see the pass coming and make a steal.

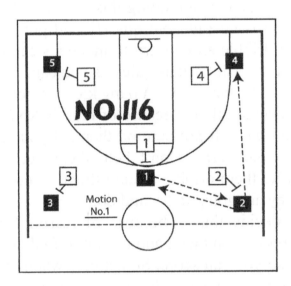

Motion No.2 Cutters (No.117)
Here are 3 of the more common moves the offense makes when they need to score from this set. Their No.1 starts to dribble around your No.1 and down the edge of the lane. Your No.1 has to go out and block them. When they see your No.1 is going to block them, they will try to pass off to their No.5 cutting to the basket. Your No.5 has to recognize this play, and move to block them, or intercept the pass. If your No.1 and No.5 players don't rotate in to block, their No.1 dribbles in for a lay-up, or short jump shot. The other play they like to run is, their No.4 cuts back towards their No.2, then when they see your No.4 over commit a little,

they cut back on the inside towards the lane, and get a pass from their No.1 while they drive to the basket for a lay-up. Your No.1, 4, and 5 players have to be watching for this, so they can move over to block it off.

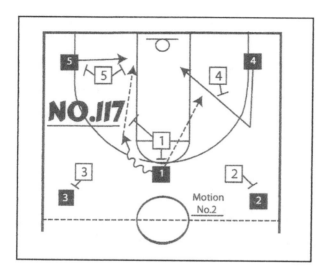

Motion No.3 Breakers & Loopers .118)
Here are 3 more offensive moves to watch for. Their No.1 passes the ball over to the wing (No.3), then breaks for the basket, stops, and loops back around to the top of the key if your No.1 follows them closely. Then if their No.3 is pressured, they pass the ball back to their No.1 at the top of the key. If your No.1 does not follow them, and your No.5 does not come part way over in the lane to block, No.1 cuts to the basket for a pass from their No.3, and goes for the lay-up. So you can see that you will have to work hard with your players to watch for, and counter this play.

If their wing players (No.2 and No.3) get pressured, either their No.4 or No.5 players will break back towards center court, to get a safety pass from their No.1. Teach your No.2, 3, 4, and 5, players to watch for this also, then move to cover. Another sneaky move the offense might try is, if either their No.2 or No.3 has the ball and they see their No.1 is pressured, they can "switch" and dribble the ball over to the top of the key, then they become the new No.1 while the first No.1 moves around in back, to the spot they just vacated on the wing. As you can see, defending the 4 corners can be hard work. You will have to have fast smart players to defend against the "4 corners".

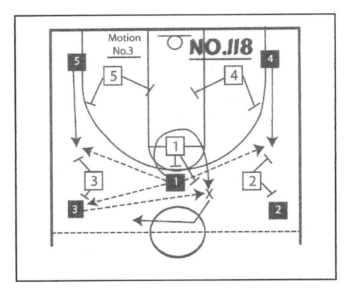

Full Court
Defensive Plays

1-2-2 Zone Press Defense
This is a pretty easy full court press to learn. And it's safe to run because it has back court coverage, to prevent lay-ups. There are 3 versions of this play you can use.
They are:

1. The **"80"** 3/4 court press with aggressive play and trapping in the back court.

2. The **"70"** press with soft pressure is designed to control the tempo of play and run time off of the clock.

3. The **"76"** which looks like the "70", but with soft pressure and an aggressive corner trap once the ball gets across the half court line.

The "80" Press
Motion No.1 (No.119)

On this press you want to tell your players to be aggressive on their play, and force the ball to the sideline and out of the middle of the court. In youth leagues the opponents No.1 (guard) usually inbounds the ball. As soon as they inbound the ball to their No.2 player your No.1 and No.2 players sprint to their No.2 player and trap them down in the corner. Your No.3 rotates across to the opposite side of the court. Your No.4 rotates over to cover, and "deny" a pass to their No.4 player. Your No.5 player drops back to prevent the long pass for a lay-up. If the opponents No.4 and 5 are switched, then your No.4 and No.5 players switch, with your No.5 covering their tallest player or center. Teach your No.4 and No.5 players to turn their bodies so that they are faced towards the sideline for steals and pass deflections. If they switch and their No.5 takes the ball out, then your No.5 has to not let a speedy guard get behind them. Teach them the CLUE is their No.1 is way up the court.

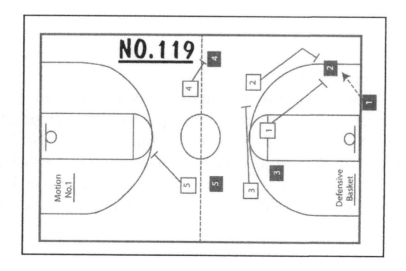

Motion No.2 (No.120)

If the ball is passed back to their No.1, your No.1 slides over a little to "deny" the pass back to their No.2. Your No.3 moves to the middle and waits until your No.2 rotates to the middle, then they slide over to the right side free throw elbow. Your No.3 does not leave the middle though until your No.2 gets there, to make sure the ball does not get up the middle of the court. Your No.4 and No.5 players rotate back to their starting positions.

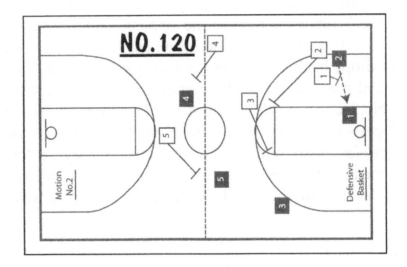

Motion No.3 (No.121)

If the ball is reversed to the opposite side of the court, your No.3 has to move over quickly, to block and prevent dribble penetration up the sideline. Your No.1 sprints over to trap, and your No.2 slides over to "deny" the middle pass. Your No.5 slides over to the ball side sideline at half court, to prevent a pass up the sideline. Your No.4 has to quickly sprint back deep as a safety, to prevent the deep pass and lay-up.

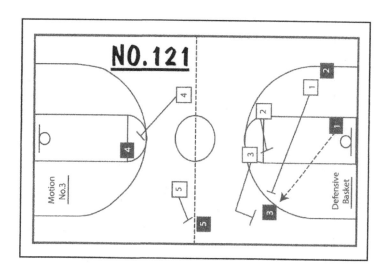

The "70'" Press (No.122)

This is more of a safe press. By that I mean soft pressure, and no trapping. It's safe because there is not much gambling, you don't give up a lay-up, and there is less chance you will foul. The whole object of this version is, slow down the offense, control the tempo, and run some time off the time clock. Your players set up just a few steps deeper than in the "80". Then they just kind of float in front of the player they are guarding, slowing up their progression up the floor.

They keep the ball in front of them, and "deny" any long passes over their head with one option. If your point guard (No.1) is very fast, quick, and aggressive, have them pressure whoever has the ball, all over the court. Your No.1 sets up first just inside of the top of the key. Your No.2 and No.3 set up just a little farther outside of the 3 point arc. Your No.4 and No.5 drop back to just in front of the 3 point arc on their end of the court. Occasionally you can spring a "trap" on them as in version "76". It works well when they think you are just laying back every time.

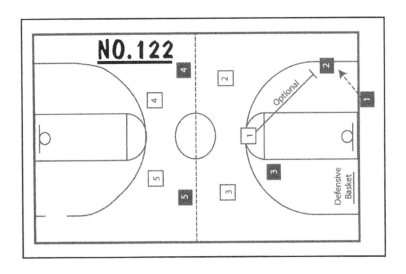

The "76" Press

Motion No.1 (No.123)

This version starts out like the "70" press with soft pressure. What you do though is, kind of lull them to sleep while your No.1 and No.2 gently steering them over to the sideline trap area. You let them come across court along the side line. Once they get across the half court line, your No.1 and No.2 players quickly move up and spring the trap on them. However if they come up the other side of the court, you can spring the trap with your No.1 and your No.3 players. Use rules then similar to the "80" press where the opposite side wing No.2 or No.3 denies the pass into the middle area. To get this play to work, your No.2 and No.3 players will have to do a little "acting". They have to act like they are just not interested in springing a trap. This is to get the ball handler to come up over the half court line into the trap box along the sideline.

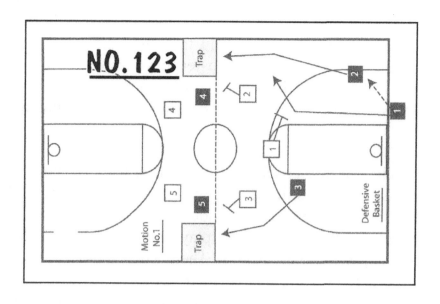

The Red "76" Press

Motion No.2 (No.124)

Your No.1, No.2, and No.3 players, depending on which side of the court the ball handler comes up on, trap them in the trap box corner. If the player they have trapped is taller, they will have to get their hands way up to block a lob pass over their heads. Have your trapping players remember, and make sure to keep their legs interlocked. Your opposite wing player No.2 or No.3 "denies" a pass back into the middle, by coming up and pressuring the closest middle of the court player to the trap box.

Your No.4 player moves to the sideline to "deny" the pass up the sideline. Your No.5 player moves over to "deny" a pass into the middle area near them. Keeping your No.5 player up near the top of the key is a gamble though because it opens the door, so to speak, for a long diagonal pass over their head to an opponent that has moved under the basket for a shot or lay-up. You probably only want to bring No.5 in once in a while as a surprise tactic.

If you keep doing it every time, eventually you will get beaten by this long pass over the top. I suggest you have a signal with your No.5 player, to let them know when you want them to come up. To make this play work, you are going to have to teach your No.2 and No.3 players to communicate with each other as to what is happening around them. Also teach your No.4 and No.5 players to communicate with each other. They have to "deny" the middle pass out from the trapped player.

A "NOTE" for you coaches that play in a league where they do not let you press. You can still set up at half court, moved back a little, and run this trap play. A little strategy note here. Coaches say there were times when they ran the "70" or "76" play just to get the ball out of the hands of their opponents best player. Then when that happened, they would switch into a "pressure man-to-man" defense, to "deny" the ball back to the opponents best player. Also coaches using this defense say many times, with young youth teams, the offense threw the ball away, and made a turnover because of the pressure and the trap.

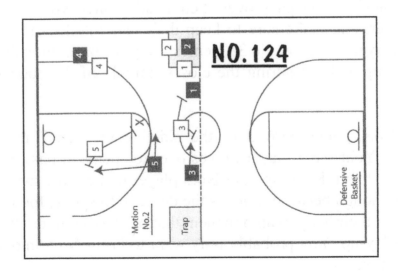

Fast Break Transition Defense

The object of this fast break transition defense is, keep the opponent from scoring an easy lay-up, or basket on the fast break. When your team shoots, at least one guard (No.1 or No.2) should not attack the boards and stay back past the 3 point circle, and in the center of the court. My suggestion is assign a certain player or players, to this position, to make sure there is no confusion who will do it.

Preventing the Fast Break (No.125)

This is basically the 2 guards back play. Have your No.1 and No.2 players stay back. When a shot goes up your No.3, No.4, and No.5 players "crash" the boards for any rebounds.

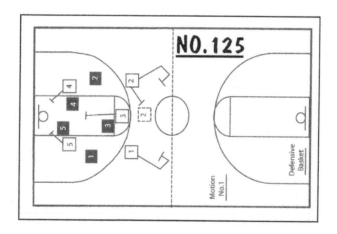

Defending the Paint Area after the Break (No.126)

If the offense gets the rebound and starts to come down the court, all your players except your No.1, sprint back down the court to around the paint area, to prevent a quick lay-up by the opposition. Your guard (No.1 or No.2) on the ball side stays back and blocks the dribbler from penetrating, or getting quickly down court. Once the fast break is stopped, all your players can go into their normal man-to-man or zone defense. If your opponent is successful in running a fast break down the court, your prevent guard (No.2) may get caught in a "2 on 1", or a "3 on 1" mismatch match.

Teach your prevent player to *first* make sure they stop the ball handler from making the lay-up. If the player decides to go for a jump shot, let them take it. It is a lower percentage shot than the lay-up. What they don't want to do is, go out away from the basket and take on the dribbler. This usually lets one of the other players slip behind them, for a pass and an easy lay-up. What they do have to do is "gap" the nearest offensive players, and how they do that is, turn sideways, try to straddle and cut off the passing lanes to the lay-up. If you can get a lot of hustle out of your team, it will stop or slow down the fast break.

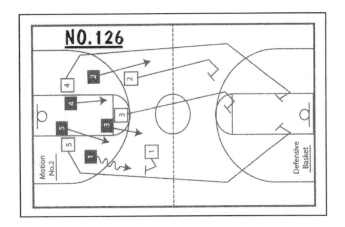

Tip Off Defense

There has to be a defense for the "tip off" if there is one, you can't just ignore it. And even though it only happens a few times a game if ever, you want to get control of the ball. Especially if you are in a championship situation, the game may be close and you want the ball. Even if the team you are playing is taller and stronger, you can still possibly cause them to make a mistake and then quickly get the ball back.

Man-to-Man Pressure "D" (No.127)

Whether they are bigger than you or not, the pressure can cause a turnover. If the offense gets the tip off, it's usually going to go to their No.4 player who is tall. If it does, their No.4 will probably try to pass it off to their No.1 or No.2 out on the wings, to get the ball down the court. Teach your players to recognize this. The second their No.4 gets the ball, your No.1 sprints out to "deny" their No.1 the pass, or if they do get the pass your No.3 comes over quickly to work a "trap" on them along with your No.1. Also if the ball goes out to their No.2 on the left wing, your No.1 goes to that side to work a "trap" with your No.2 on them.

If their No.4 holds the ball or dribbles down the lane, your No.4 either goes directly over to pressure them, or sprints down into the lane ahead of them to block them. While all of this is going on, your No.2 sprints over to cover and "deny" their No.2 the pass. Their No.5 center will probably head for the lo-post after tipping to No.4. Your No.5 has to recognize this, and immediately sprint out ahead of their No.5 to "deny" them a pass. If the tip off goes behind to their No.3 player, your No.3 has to quickly move forward, to block and pressure them from penetrating into the front court. Also make sure to teach your players not to foul the opposing player while they are pressuring them.

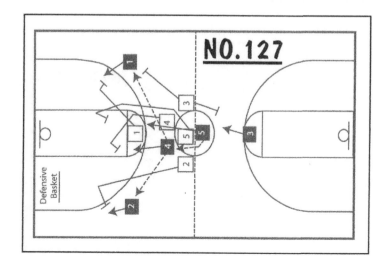

9. Defensive Training Games

Note: ALL ACTIVITIES will be numbered for "EASY " reference.

These are games you can have your team play once in a while. This will break up the practice from endless hours of drills. The kids are learning a defensive skill they can use, but having a little fun while playing the game.

Skill Activity No. 156- *The Ball Scramble Game*
The Object of the game is: Players learn how to develop their skills for get to loose balls, and learn how to move quickly without the ball.
What you will need to play the game:
You will need 1 basketball for every player, 2 coaches, and a whistle.
The Basics of the game are:
All players get a ball and go to the key circle in the middle of half court. On a whistle they all drop their ball and run to the half court center line or whatever area they are sent to. They make a one hand touch there and run back (scramble) to the key circle and grab a ball. Each time the players are running one ball is removed from center court. This means one player won't have a ball when they get back. That player is out of the game. This keeps going on until only one player is left with a ball. That player wins the game.

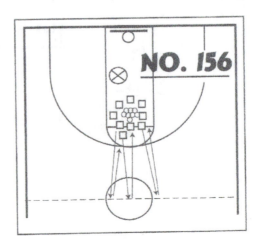

How to play the game:

Here is how it works. All players take their ball to center court. Coach blows the whistle and all players drop their ball and run to the designated area (a line or the bleachers) and touch one hand down. Then they run back to center court and grab a ball. Then coach blows the whistle and it starts over again. When it gets down to the last two players, when they touch down and scramble back only one will have a ball. That player wins. There is no pushing, shoving, or fighting over balls. The first player to it gets the ball. If players don't touch a hand down or they foul another player trying to get a ball, a ball is removed, and they are out of the game, and the appropriate number of balls are removed so that there is always one less ball than the number of players left in the game, Coaches make sure nobody cheats.

How long to play the game:

The game runs until there is a winner or 30 minutes whichever comes first

How to make the game easier or harder:

I would use the centerline to touch down for the real little kids.

Skill Activity No. 157- *The Ball Steal Game*

The Object of the game is: Players learn how to develop their skills for stealing the ball away from the dribbler, without fouling, by using quick hands.

What you will need to play the game:

You will need 1 basketball, some cones to mark the boundary lines, 2 coaches, and a whistle.

The Basics of the game are: Your team is split in two groups, half the group on one side of the court, the other half on the opposite side of the court. While staying in their defensive area the defensive players try to steal the ball as the dribbler goes by them. If the defender steals the ball their team gets 2 points, if they can knock it away its 1 point. Then the groups trade places and the dribblers become the defenders. The idea is to get the most points by stealing the ball. At the end of the game the team with the most points wins the game. Players are rotated after two runs.

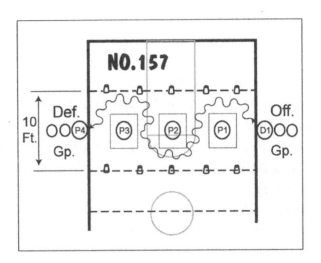

How to play the game:

Here is how it works. The team is split up into two equal size groups, one on each side of the court. The group starting with "D1" attempts to weave dribble around the defensive players "P1-P3." P1 –P3 must stay inside of a 4 foot square box area, with a 3 foot clearance on both sides marking the boundary lines, and try to steal the ball from the dribbler or knock it away with their hands. Their feet must stay in the box, but their hands can extend over. Mark the defenders boxes with white tape. They are not allowed to foul though. The boundary lines are marked with orange cones. If they steal the ball or knock it away their team gets points and the run stops with a whistle. Teams switch after 2 runs, and the dribbler team becomes the defender ball steal team. The rules are the dribbler has to run the gauntlet, but it can be at varying speeds, and they can use any type of dribble they like, between the legs, behind the back, or whatever. Don't forget to rotate the players after 2 runs. One coach keeps the score on a pad of paper.

How long to play the game:

Play the game for 30 minutes with each team getting an equal number of times as the stealers.

How to make the game easier or harder:

For the little kids you may need to change the clearance area on both sides of the box to 2 feet wide to make it easier. For the bigger kids if the steals are too easy you may need to adjust the clearance area on both sides to 4 feet wide.

Skill Activity No. 160- The Steal the Bacon Game

The Object of the game is:

Players learn how to develop their skills for stealing the ball away from the dribbler, without fouling, by using quick hands.

The Basics of the game are:

Here is how it works. This is a little game you can play to help your players learn to make steals, and to shield the ball. You can play this game 2 vs 1 or 1 vs 1, or both ways by alternating (best). P2 and/or P3 attempt to steal the ball from P1 as they dribble between them and attempt to shoot a basket.

What you will need to play the game:

You will need 1 basketball, 2 coaches, and a whistle.

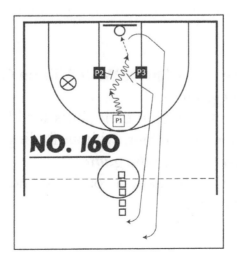

NO. 160

How to play the game:

Line your team up back at the at the half court line. Your first player goes to the top of the key with a basketball. Then one or two defenders go to the edges of the lane. On your whistle P1 has one minute to dribble through the defenders and attempt to take a shot at the basket. Blow your whistle after one minute is up. You may need to go to two minutes for the real little kids. If P1 can't break through the two players then go 1 vs 1 (P1,P2). If P1 can break through, give them one point. If they make the basket, give them two points. Have one of your assistant coaches keep score in a notebook. If P2 or P3 can steal the ball cleanly, give them two points. If they can knock the ball away, give them one point. However, they can not touch the dribbler's arms at any point in the attempt (fouling). If the stealer fouls they get no points. Make sure that everyone gets a chance to play the offensive and defensive positions. The player with the most points wins the game.

How long to play the game:

I would play the game no longer than one 30 minutes then move on to something else. Here is an idea. Break your team up into two groups. The other group can be working on something else at the other end of the court. This way everyone keeps busy and more learning is accomplished.

How to make the game easier or harder:

If it's too hard for the little kids then bring the stealers in a little closer together. If it's too easy for the bigger kids move the stealers farther apart.

Skill Activity No. 161- The "SWAT" Team Game

The Object of the game is:

Players learn how to develop their skills for blocking shots and swatting the ball away from the dribbler, without fouling, by using quick hands.

What you will need to play the game:

You will need 1 basketball, 1 or 2 defenders, 1 dribbler/shooter, 2 coaches, and a whistle.

The Basics of the game are:

Here is how it works. This is a little game you can play to help your players learn to make blocks and swat the ball away. You can play this game 2 vs 1 or 1 vs 1 or both ways by alternating (best). S1 dribbles up to a line about 5 feet past the free throw line which is marked with orange cones, stops and makes a baby jumper shot. P2 and/or P3 come in, jump up, and attempt to block the shot or swat it away.

How to play the game:

Line your team up back at the at the half court line. Your first player goes to the top of the key at the free throw line with a basketball. Then one or two defenders go to the edges of the lane. On your whistle S1 dribbles in to the shooting line and attempts to make a baby jumper shot. On the whistle the defender(s) attacks the shooting line and the dribbler and attempts to block or SWAT the ball. If they block the shot they get 2 points. If they swat the ball away or just get their hand on it they get 1 point. If the shooter makes the basket they get 1 point. Rotate the defenders after 2 attempts. The last defender(s) go to the end of the shooters line when they are done. The shooters go to the end of the defenders line when they are done. This way everyone gets to try blocking or swatting. The player with the most points at the end of the game wins. One coach keeps track of the score on a pad of paper.

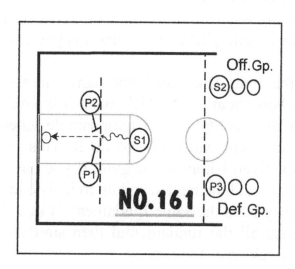

How long to play the game:

I would play the game no longer than 30 minutes then move on to something else. Here is an idea. Break your team up into two groups. The other group can be working on something else at the other end of the court. This way everyone keeps busy and more learning is accomplished.

How to make the game easier or harder:

If it's too hard for the little kids then bring the blockers/swatters in a little closer together. If it's too easy for the bigger kids move the stealers farther apart or farther away from the shooter.

10. Typical Practice Schedules

Why Have Practice Schedules

When you lay out a practice schedule, kids learn more, and faster (Practice is usually 1 hour for beginners). You can't always follow it to the letter, but you try to follow it as close as possible within reason. I know many of you coaches don't like to follow a schedule, but if you do, you are going to find that the kids learn a lot more, do it quicker, and their skills improve much faster. The secret is plan out what you want to teach each session, the get some assistant coaches to help, as many as possible. They can even be parents, who may just be sitting around doing nothing watching anyway, might as well put them to work. It's not hard if you just show them EXACTLY what it is you want them to do.

I do this all the time. And I find that many parents are willing to help as long as you show them EXACTLY what it is you want them to do. We will put some different types of 1 hour sample schedules together for you to see some different ways how to do it. This is because most young teams are only given 1 hour in the gym. If you have more than an hour to practice then just add the next schedule to it. The idea is to show you how to teach larger groups the same fundamentals in 3 days instead of 4 or 5. After you teach all the fundamental then start the drills over again by selecting the weak areas to work on.

1 Hour Sample Schedules

METHOD 1- BEGINNERS
(Smaller Groups of up to 9)
Practice 1 (One Coach, One Asst.)

Coach Plus Asst. (Whole Group)
4:00 to 4:10 Stretching and Exercising (All Together)
4:10 to 4:20 Defensive Stance Drill
4:20 to 4:25 Water Break
4:25 to 4:35 Shuffle Slide Step Drill
4:35 to 4:45 Boxing Out Drill
4:45 to 4:50 Water Break
4:50 to 5:00 Guarding the Dribbler Drill
5:00 to 5:05 End of Practice Closure (All Together)

Practice 2 (One Coach, One Asst.)

Coach Plus Asst. (Whole Group)
4:00 to 4:10 Stretching and Exercising (All Together)
4:10 to 4:20 Guarding the Shooter Drill
4:20 to 4:25 Water Break
4:25 to 4:35 Shooting Guard Man-To-Man Responsibilities Drill
4:35 to 4:45 Guards Man-To-Man Rotating Drill
4:45 to 4:50 Water Break
4:50 to 5:00 Guards Man-To-Man Converging Drill
5:00 to 5:05 End of Practice Closure (All Together)

METHOD 2- BEGINNERS
(For Large Groups of 10 to 20)
Practice 1 (One Coach, One Assistant)

Note: Split into Two Groups
4:00 to 4:10 Stretching and Exercising (All Together)

Coach- Group 1
4:10 to 4:20 Small Forward Man-To-Man Responsibilities Drill
4:20 to 4:25 Water Break
4:25 to 4:35 Power Forward Man-To-Man Responsibilities Drill
4:35 to 4:45 Center Man-To-Man Responsibilities Drill
4:45 to 4:50 Water Break
4:50 to 5:00 Man-To-Man Screen Responsibilities Drill
5:00 to 5:05 End of Practice Closure (All Together)

Assistant- Group 2 (Simultaneously)
4:10 to 4:20 General Shot Blocking Drill
4:20 to 4:25 Water Break
4:25 to 4:35 General Making Steals Drill
4:35 to 4:45 Man-To-Man Rebounding Drill
4:45 to 4:50 Water Break
4:50 to 5:00 General Diving For Loose Balls Drill
5:00 to 5:05 End of Practice Closure (All Together)

Practice 2 (One Coach, One Assistant)
Note: Still Split into Two Groups
4:00 to 4:10 Stretching and Exercising (All Together)
Coach- Group 2
4:10 to 4:20 Small Forward Man-To-Man Responsibilities Drill
4:20 to 4:25 Water Break
4:25 to 4:35 Power Forward Man-To-Man Responsibilities Drill
4:35 to 4:45 Center Man-To-Man Responsibilities Drill
4:45 to 4:50 Water Break
4:50 to 5:00 Man-To-Man Screen Responsibilities Drill
5:00 to 5:05 End of Practice Closure (All Together)

Assistant- Group 1 (Simultaneously)
4:10 to 4:20 General Shot Blocking Drill
4:20 to 4:25 Water Break
4:25 to 4:35 General Making Steals Drill
4:35 to 4:45 Man-To-Man Rebounding Drill
4:45 to 4:50 Water Break
4:50 to 5:00 General Diving For Loose Balls Drill
5:00 to 5:05 End of Practice Closure (All Together)

METHOD 3- BEGINNERS
(For Large Groups of 10 to 20)

Practice 1 (One Coach, One Assistant)
Note: Split into Two Groups
4:00 to 4:10 Stretching and Exercising (All Together)
Coach- Group 1
4:10 to 4:20 Guards in a 2-3 Zone Defense Drill
4:20 to 4:25 Water Break

4:25 to 5:00 The Ball Scramble Game on One End of the Court
5:00 to 5:05 End of Practice Closure (All Together)

Assistant- Group 2 (Simultaneously)
4:10 to 4:20 Forwards in a 2-3 Zone Drill
4:20 to 4:25 Water Break
4:25 to 5:00 The Ball Scramble Game on the Other End of the Court
5:00 to 5:05 End of Practice Closure (All Together)

Practice 2 (One Coach, One Assistant)
Note: Split into Two Groups
4:00 to 4:10 Stretching and Exercising (All Together)
Coach- Group 1
4:10 to 4:20 Centers in a 2-3 Zone Defense Drill
4:20 to 4:25 Water Break
4:25 to 5;00 The "SWAT" Team Game (All Together or at one end of the court)
5:00 to 5:05 End of Practice Closure (All Together)

Assistant- Group 2 (Simultaneously)
4:10 to 4:20 Other Zone Defenses Drill
4:20 to 4:25 Water Break
4:25 to 5;00 The "SWAT" Team Game (All Together or at the other end of the court)
5:00 to 5:05 End of Practice Closure (All Together)

METHOD 4- BEGINNERS
(For Large Groups of up to 30)

Practice 1 (Multiple Coaches- Stations- Groups Rotate From 1-2-3)
Note: Split into Three Groups
4:00 to 4:10 Stretching and Exercising (All Together)
Head Coach- Group 1
4:10 to 4:20 Defensive Stance Drill
4:20 to 4:25 Water Break
4:25 to 4:35 Shuffle Slide Step Drill
4:35 to 4:45 Boxing Out Drill
4:45 to 4:50 Water Break
4:50 to 5:00 Guarding the Dribbler Drill
5:00 to 5:05 End of Practice Closure (All Together)

Assistant- Group 2 (Simultaneously)
4:10 to 4:20 Guarding the Shooter Drill
4:20 to 4:25 Water Break
4:25 to 4:35 Shooting Guard Man-To-Man Responsibilities Drill
4:35 to 4:45 Guards Man-To-Man Rotating Drill
4:45 to 4:50 Water Break
4:50 to 5:00 Guards Man-To-Man Converging Drill
5:00 to 5:05 End of Practice Closure (All Together)

Assistant- Group 3 (Simultaneously)
4:10 to 4:20 Small Forward Man-To-Man Responsibilities Drill
4:20 to 4:25 Water Break
4:25 to 4:35 Power Forward Man-To-Man Responsibilities Drill
4:35 to 4:45 Center Man-To-Man Responsibilities Drill
4:45 to 4:50 Water Break
4:50 to 5:00 Man-To-Man Screen Responsibilities Drill
5:00 to 5:05 End of Practice Closure (All Together)

Practice 2 (Multiple Coaches- Stations- Groups Rotate From 1-2-3)

Note: Split into the Same Three Groups
4:00 to 4:10 Stretching and Exercising (All Together)
Head Coach- Group 3
4:10 to 4:20 Defensive Stance Drill
4:20 to 4:25 Water Break
4:25 to 4:35 Shuffle Slide Step Drill
4:35 to 4:45 Boxing Out Drill
4:45 to 4:50 Water Break
4:50 to 5:00 Guarding the Dribbler Drill
5:00 to 5:05 End of Practice Closure (All Together)

Assistant- Group 1 (Simultaneously)
4:10 to 4:20 Guarding the Shooter Drill
4:20 to 4:25 Water Break
4:25 to 4:35 Shooting Guard Man-To-Man Responsibilities Drill
4:35 to 4:45 Guards Man-To-Man Rotating Drill
4:45 to 4:50 Water Break
4:50 to 5:00 Guards Man-To-Man Converging Drill
5:00 to 5:05 End of Practice Closure (All Together)

138

Assistant- Group 2 (Simultaneously)
4:10 to 4:20 Small Forward Man-To-Man Responsibilities Drill
4:20 to 4:25 Water Break
4:25 to 4:35 Power Forward Man-To-Man Responsibilities Drill
4:35 to 4:45 Center Man-To-Man Responsibilities Drill
4:45 to 4:50 Water Break
4:50 to 5:00 Man-To-Man Screen Responsibilities Drill
5:00 to 5:05 End of Practice Closure (All Together)

Practice 3 (Multiple Coaches- Stations- Groups Rotate From 1-2-3)

Note: Split into The Same Three Groups
4:00 to 4:10 Stretching and Exercising (All Together)
Head Coach- Group 2
4:10 to 4:20 Defensive Stance Drill
4:20 to 4:25 Water Break
4:25 to 4:35 Shuffle Slide Step Drill
4:35 to 4:45 Boxing Out Drill
4:45 to 4:50 Water Break
4:50 to 5:00 Guarding the Dribbler Drill
5:00 to 5:05 End of Practice Closure (All Together)

Assistant- Group 3 (Simultaneously)
4:10 to 4:20 Guarding the Shooter Drill
4:20 to 4:25 Water Break
4:25 to 4:35 Shooting Guard Man-To-Man Responsibilities Drill
4:35 to 4:45 Guards Man-To-Man Rotating Drill
4:45 to 4:50 Water Break
4:50 to 5:00 Guards Man-To-Man Converging Drill
5:00 to 5:05 End of Practice Closure (All Together)

Assistant- Group 1 (Simultaneously)
4:10 to 4:20 Small Forward Man-To-Man Responsibilities Drill
4:20 to 4:25 Water Break
4:25 to 4:35 Power Forward Man-To-Man Responsibilities Drill
4:35 to 4:45 Center Man-To-Man Responsibilities Drill
4:45 to 4:50 Water Break
4:50 to 5:00 Man-To-Man Screen Responsibilities Drill
5:00 to 5:05 End of Practice Closure (All Together)

Scheduling Summation

There are all kinds of ways to set up training. And they may all work, but some ways are better than others because they are more efficient. Also progression is probably a better way to go. In other words start with what fundamental skill they need to know first before they start the next one. Also it may be a good idea to have the coach one day, and the assistant the next day, teaching the same skill. It's like batting in baseball, some kids will catch on with one particular technique over another, and be successful with it. Such as how they swing the bat or how they pitch. So maybe another coaches technique will help a young beginner learn how to do something in another way that will make them successful.

Note:

In 3 days or practices up to 30 kids may have been taught all the above different fundamental techniques shown.

What is "**End of Practice Closure**?" You have all your kids come together then go quickly over how the days practice went. Tell them they did an awesome job. Give them any reminders or notices. Then all the players get in a big circle together with a hand up in the middle all touching. Then coach says, "One two three" and everyone yells "Yeah Team" or whatever they want to yell. This way kids all go home on a good note.

11. Special Skills Training

Why Have Special Skills Training

These are drills that will give your players extra agility, coordination and speed to help them become better basketball players.

Drills for Jumping

Skill Activity (No.162) Over the Broomstick

Object of the activity:

Teach all your players how to get more straight up jumping ability with a little forward motion.

What you will need:

You will need only a corner area of the court, a group of players, a broomstick, 1 coach, and a whistle.

The Basics Are:

Jumping over an object will train the leg muscles, to get high up in the air going forward. This drill is not very complicated, but it should help them some with getting the feeling of getting up in the air. No special training equipment is used just an ordinary broom. Players line up in front of the broom. On the whistle players jump over the broomstick handle and go to the end of the line.

Working the activity:

Just take a regular broom, and use the handle as a bar, for them to get their feet over. You hold the broom, and have them stand stationary about 18 inches in front of the broom handle. Next, in one jump, have them jump up over the handle and land on the other side on both feet *(SEE FIGURE 162).* All players should learn how to build up their jumping muscles, but make sure all your "Centers" and "Power Forwards" work on this drill. You can start with 5 year olds by raising the handle to about 8 inches off the floor, through 12 year olds at about 12 inches off the floor. They should start out by doing about 5 of these each day. You can increase the number of repetitions, and raise the handle higher and higher as they get a little older and stronger, and better at doing it. A *TIP* here is, have them swing their arms down and bend their knees a little just before jumping up. Kind of like the standing broad jump

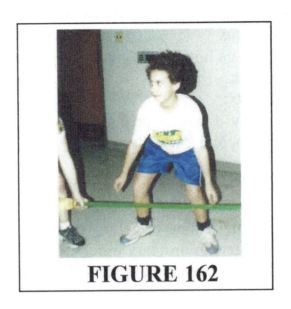
FIGURE 162

Emphasize:

To your players that they need to dip their knees and swing their arms to get their upward momentum going.

Run this activity:

At team practice for about 10 minutes, making sure each player gets at least 2 attempts at jumping the broomstick. If players are not catching on then you or an assistant coach pull them aside and show them what they are doing wrong so that the practice does not stop and keeps going.

Skill Activity (No.163) Grab the Flag

Object of the activity:

Teach all your players how to get more straight up jumping ability like for rebounding.

What you will need:

You will need only a corner area of the court, a group of players, a broomstick, a handkerchief or bandana,1 coach, and a whistle.

The Basics Are:

This is a jumping way up and reaching drill that will help them improve on their jumping straight up ability as well as their reach for rebounds ability. It will also help centers get up in the air higher, to block shots. The idea is, make it into a habit for them to jump up, and not stand flat footed on the floor and wait for the ball to come down. All players should learn how to jump up and reach, but make sure all your "Centers" and "Power Forwards" really work hard on this drill.

Working the activity:

Take the same broom, an old rag or bandana (the Flag) and stick the rag into the bristles, just enough to hold it in place. Then you, or a player, hold the broom and the flag, way up in the air. Have your players stand directly underneath the flag then on the whistle jump straight up, and try to grab the flag first with either hand, then with two hands. Watch how far their feet get up off the floor, then once they get up high enough to grab it, then keep raising the flag just a little bit, out of there reach, so they have to keep getting up higher to grab it *(SEE FIGURE 163).* They should start out by doing 2 of these with *each* hand then you can increase the number a little as they get older and stronger, and better at getting higher off the floor. A *TIP* here is, have them push off with their left foot when just the right hand goes up, and push off with the right foot when just the left hand goes up. A coach should try to keep track of their height off the floor in a little book so you will be able to see improvement.

FIGURE 163

Emphasize:

To your players that they need to dip their knees a little and drive the push off foot up hard to get the upward momentum going.

Run this activity:

At team practice for about 10 minutes, making sure each player gets at least 2 attempts at grabbing the flag. If players are not catching on then you or an assistant coach pull them aside and show them what they are doing wrong so that the practice does not stop and keeps going.

Drills for Coordination and Agility

These drills are designed to teach your players how to move around on their feet better, without falling down (mobility). These drills will also help them improve their balance and agility. If you players will do these drills every day, even for a short while, you will notice their coordination and agility improving after just a few weeks.

Skill Activity (No.164) Crossover Foot Drill

Object of the activity:

Teach all your players how to improve on their mobility in all directions.

What you will need:

You will need a full court, a group of players, 1 coach, and a whistle.

The Basics Are:

This is called the crossover foot, and side to side, exercise drill. The feet have to keep crossing over each other, from in front to behind going sideways. The arms are held out to the sides for balance. It's an old football drill, but it works great for coordination and agility training in any sport. All position players need to work on this drill.

Working the activity:

Take your players out to the width of half the court, to the park, or in their back yard where there is grass and lots of room. They will need grass and lots of room because they will be moving side to side for about 40 or 50 yards outdoors, the grass will help cushion them if they fall. And they usually do that a lot at first. Stand in front of them and face each other at about three yards apart. You do the same steps they do and both of you need to be moving in the same direction. Start out both of you walking through this slowly until they can learn how to move their feet. Then speed up little by little until you both get better at it. Start with the feet apart, then have them step to their left with their left foot.

Next step to the left, with their right foot crossing over the top of their left foot. Then step again to the left, with their left foot crossing behind their right foot. Next step again to the left, with the right foot crossing behind their left foot. Then step again to the left, with the left foot over the top of the right foot. Then keep repeating this combination of steps to the left, over and over, down the court. Then stop at the end of the court and reverse all these steps, going to their right, first with their left foot over their right foot, and so on, for about 30 yards to the right. Keeping their hands straight out to their sides will help them keep their balance. The better they get at doing this, you can speed the process up little by little. After a few weeks your players or kids should be able to do this drill on the run, and without falling down. If not, keep working with them and don't give up because they can learn to do it. *(SEE FIGURE164).*

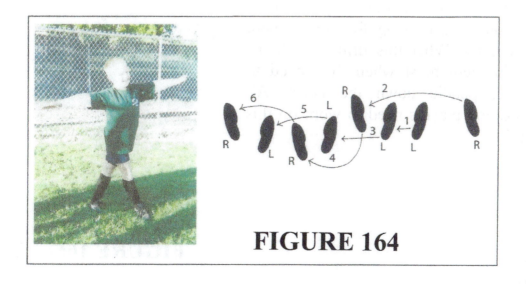

FIGURE 164

Emphasize:

To your players that they need to focus on what their feet need to do, and keep their arms out at their sides for balance.

Run this activity:

At team practice for about 10 minutes, making sure all players get to work on this for the whole drill period. They can work on this back and forth for about 3 or 4 minutes, rest a minute or two then continue for another 3 or 4 minutes. If your little beginning kids, or other beginning players, are NOT catching on how to do this with their feet then you or an assistant coach pull them aside and show them what they are doing wrong so that the practice does not stop and keeps going.

Skill Activity (No.165) The Running Backwards Drill

Object of the activity:

Teach all your players how to improve on their mobility going backwards then changing to running forward without stopping.

What you will need:

You will need the full court, a group of players, 1 coach, and a whistle.

The Basics Are:

This is called the running backwards coordination drill. It is running backwards with the feet and arms pumping up and down then turning around and running forward without stopping. What this drill will do is, help them most when they need to back peddle down the court. All position players need to work on this drill.

FIGURE 165

Working the activity:

You will need the full court to work on this in the gym, or you will need to find a very large back yard, or a big area in a park with thick grass if they are working on this at home. The reason I am suggesting thick grass is it will help cushion their fall a little if they fall backwards. You will have to do a walk through then go slow at first because there is a danger of falling backwards, and getting whip lash to the neck and head. First both you in front of them and all your players line up and face you side by side at one end of the court, with about 3 yards between them, and some clear space all the way down the court behind you. Then all of you start slowly jogging backwards while pumping your arms up and down. Do this all the way down to the other end of the court, then stop, turn around, and repeat the drill going backwards down the court the other way to where you started.

Usually some will fall down the first few times they try this drill, especially 5 or 6 year old kids. If any of them fall down stop the drill, have everyone re-line up, and continue running backwards. A warning, if you criticize them too much, they may not want to do it any more. If you are doing this at home and your son or daughter is falling down, and you are not, then you may want to fall down a few times yourself on purpose. This is so they will think that it is hard for you also, and they won't get discouraged. This usually works in keeping them interested. This is just at home though. Also shout encouragement to them as you are running side by side with them. The secret for keeping your balance is, raising your knees up high while pumping your hands up and down as fast as you can. Once they can run fast all the way down the court, and not fall down, you will notice their interest level go up.

When they do become good at this, then you can change the drill a little to make it harder. A suggestion on how to do this might be, have them run backwards about 5 yards then blow a whistle, then have them turn around without stopping, and run forward in the same direction for another 5 yards. Keep doing this, and change directions, all the way down the court. This drill alone is one of the best drills for kids that I have ever seen, that will really improve on their coordination and agility up and down the court *(SEE FIGURE 165)*.

Emphasize:

To your players that they need to focus on what their feet and arms are doing for balance.

Run this activity:

At team practice for about 10 minutes, making sure all players get to work on this for the whole drill period. They can work on this back and forth for about 3 or 4 minutes, rest a minute or two then continue for another 3 or 4 minutes. If your little beginning kids, or players, are NOT catching on how to do this with their feet then you or an assistant coach pull them aside and show them what they are doing wrong so that the practice does not stop and keeps going.

THE END

CPSIA information can be obtained at www.ICGtesting.com
Printed in the USA
LVOW02s1625180514

386227LV00001B/1/P